8 Excellent Marriage

A Training Manual to Equip You in Discovering God's Grand Design

Craig Debinski
with Pamela Debinski

TIMELESS TEXTS
WOODRUFF, SC

Contents

Foreword

The book *Excellent Marriage*, by Craig Debinski, is a useful tool that engaged or married couples will find helpful. This "training manual" is *just that* – it seeks to inculcate Scriptural principles in a practical way. It provides grist for a fruitful Bible study and information for engaged couples, and would be a helpful "refresher course" for any married couple. It is down-to-earth, easy to understand and use, and is *biblical*. The scope is wide, but the content is not shallow. You will soon find yourself recommending this book to others.

Jay E. Adams
Enoree, SC 2001

Acknowledgments

The Scripture teaches that "Iron sharpeneth iron; so a man sharpeneth the countenance of his friend" (Proverbs 27:17). God has raised up Christian friends in my life, and I cannot thank them enough. Like Barnabas, these saints have ministered to my needs time and time again.

My journey has been long and not without deep potholes. In 1969, I was searching for answers to life, but found none. Life was futile! God sent Ed Hommerbocker in 1972, and he loved me like a brother. Through him I met Jim Winslow, who became my spiritual father. Jim spiritually challenged me in a home Bible study, and as a result I trusted in Christ on April 23, 1973. In 1975, I was troubled over a Church problem, and God provided refreshment and renewal through pastors Cal Thomas and George Smith. These men were like Elisha and Elijah to me, and I am writing this today because of their loving ministry to me.

The late Dr. Watson Pindell demonstrated Christianity to my fiancée and me as we listened to his premarital counsel at Washington Bible College in 1976. After completing J. Allan Petersen's "Two Become One" study, my fiancée and I wed on June 18, 1977. God used many men and women to bless and encourage us through the years, and I'm looking forward to personally thanking them when we all sit around the table together at the Marriage Supper of the Lamb.

I served alongside Dr. Charles Zimmerman from 1988–92 in Brooklyn, New York. He modeled practical faith that showed me how the Bible can shape the way we respond to "well-intentioned dragons." Since 1992, I have served as the pastor of Temple Baptist Church in New Jersey. It's small, but sincere; struggling, but striving to please Jesus Christ. Many great things have occurred, and a special thank you is warmly sent to the Charter and Board members of Temple Baptist Church. The Board members who served during my ministry include the late Tom Burns, the late Jerry Greaux, Daniel Holt, Daniel Hedberg, Ernest Posik, and Greg Cannonie. Charter members include Mary Hacku (Posik), Helen Bartus (Staniszewski), Esther Zigre (Gerak), and Betty Kolator (Gerak).

My greatest encourager is my partner and life companion, Pamela Sue. I am blessed to have married such an example of godly woman-hood. Her tender patience and continuous support have enabled me to buck hurricane winds and walk through spiritual mine fields. God has been better to me than I deserve. No one needs to remind me of how blessed I am. I know! *Thank you, dear God.*

The Reader and the Writer

The Reader

This manual is designed for you to complete the questions and then discuss your responses in a Bible study or a premarital session. If you are engaged, your minister may assign a mentoring couple to you, or he may lead you through this study himself. If you are completing this for a Bible study, then the group leader will discuss your answers within your small group meeting. At the end of each chapter is a page entitled "Personal Reflections." This is so you may make a note of your thoughts after the Bible study or counseling session has ended.

Although you could benefit from completing it on your own without a mentoring couple or counselor, you and your partner will spiritually profit the most through the suggested format.

As readers, each one of you is unique. This manual is written as a practical resource. The lists of resources at the end of each chapter are purposefully extensive so one may gain the maximum exposure to available materials on each subject. I recommend this equipping tool to:

- **Engaged Couples** who want to prepare for marriage.
- **Married Couples** who desire to improve their marriage.
- **Home** or **Church Bible Studies, Cell Groups, Sunday School Classes,** or **Marriage Retreats**.
- **Parents**. You may have been married for years and now you are going to be parents again or maybe for the first time. This refresher course will help you to set and keep priorities in the right order.
- **Remarried or Remarrying Couples.** Maybe you were married for years but now you are remarrying. If so, this training manual will help. Don't be like the groom who had a hard time getting a minister to tie-the-knot without his having had premarital counseling. He complained, "What do I need premarital counseling for? I've already been married five times."

The Writer

I have been privileged to learn under the tutelage of great teachers at Washington Bible College (BA), Biblical Theological Seminary (MA), the Graduate School of Pensacola Christian College (Ph.D., ABD), and The Christian Counseling and Educational Foundation (*Competent to Counsel* and *The Graduate Studies in Pastoral Counseling* certificates). I am grateful to the leaders who equipped me to serve Christ in his Church. Special thanks to Doctors Jim Schuppe, William Miller, and George Miles from WBC; Wayne Mack, Ed Welch, Jay Adams, Earl Cook, John Bettler, and David Powlison from (CCEF); David Dunbar, Fred Putnam, and Charles Zimmerman from (BTS); and Arlin and Beka Horton, Greg Mutsch, Joel Mullenix, Dell Johnson, Harry Nonnemacher and John Reese from Pensacola Christian College.

Introduction

Everybody wants to be happily married. Advice columnists offer suggestions everyday in most major newspapers. But all marriages do not last. According to *World* Magazine, the former Chicago Bull Dennis Rodman may hold the record for being married the shortest length of time. He married Carmen Electra on November 14, 1998, separated from her the same day, and filed an annulment nine days later.[1] The two officially filed for divorce on April 6, 1999.[2] But what makes marriages last for a lifetime?

Laura Morice, a secular writer for *Redbook* magazine, offers nine suggestions in her article "Marriage Resolutions for the New Year."[3] She recommends, "Be your spouse's biggest fan, bring something new to sex, be kind, spend quality time apart, spend quality time together, put it in writing, break the date rut, make a five-year plan, and do that one task your spouse has been bugging you about." Some of these common sense ideas might be helpful, but are they enough to achieve a mutually satisfying marriage? There must be more to it than that!

Stephen R. Covey, a popular writer who is also a Mormon, in "Why Character Counts: Without it, You'll Never Truly Succeed," relates the story of an unfaithful bank president and the morale problem it caused. The bank president's mistress was a bank employee in the same branch. As a consultant hired to discover and repair the morale problem, Covey confronted the bank president, who ended the affair and admitted his infidelity to his wife and his staff. Covey concludes, "It took time, but eventually employee morale – a sense of openness, optimism and trust – improved. In the end, however, the executive was doing himself the greatest favor. He was finding his own path to character."[4]

While this is a warm story about a man who took responsibility for his sin, it also is a clear statement that the answer to immorality is character. Is it? If everyone had more character, would all marriages succeed? Covey explains that character, which he considers very important, is made up of such traits as integrity, honesty, courage, fairness and generosity – which arise from the hard choices we have to make in life. But is character enough?

Covey's answer, like many others, is inadequate. The answer to lasting marriages lies in the creator of marriage. Since God created love, sex, and marriage, He holds the answers to their design. A sincere study of God's wisdom on marriage is the wisest investment any couple could make. The proper study of God's wisdom will bring forth practical insights which, when applied, will lead to a successful marriage. The application of this material may be your best preparation for a rewarding and happy marriage.

Foundations for Marriage

Study One

YOUR QUALIFICATIONS

In order to be united together in Christian marriage, spiritual qualifications need to be considered. Both partners must be Christians. The designation "Christian" is used to mean different things to different people. Evangelist Luis Palau answers the question, "What is a Real Christian?" by exposing ten myths about what makes someone a Christian. He probes,

> Maybe you were raised in a Catholic or Protestant home. Or maybe you were brought up in some other religion. And you tell yourself, "Well, I think I'm all right. Don't worry about me." No matter what your background, I encourage you to take an honest look – beyond the myths – about what makes someone a Christian.[5]

What are the ten myths? Evangelist Palau identifies them as
Myth # 1: Being Born in America Makes You a Christian;
Myth # 2: Thinking Positively Makes You A Christian;
Myth # 3: Living a Good Life Makes You a Christian;
Myth # 4: Going to Church Makes You a Christian;
Myth # 5: Giving to Others Makes You a Christian;
Myth # 6: Receiving a Sacrament Makes You a Christian;
Myth # 7: Believing in God Makes You a Christian;
Myth # 8: Talking About Jesus Christ Makes You a Christian;
Myth # 9: Praying Makes You a Christian;
Myth #10: Reading the Bible Makes You a Christian.[6]

What is a Christian? A Christian is a person who takes responsibility for his sin and repents (Acts 2:36–41). This means he is remorseful for grieving God due to his inner rebellion (Ephesians 4:30), and he confesses his iniquity and is forgiven (1 John 1:9). Furthermore, a Christian humbles himself and declares his personal faith in Jesus Christ (Acts 8:26–38, 16:30–34). He is spiritually baptized by the

1

Holy Spirit, who indwells him and places him into the Body of Christ (Romans 6:3–10, Ephesians 1:13–14, 1 Corinthians 12:13–14). A Christian is not perfect, but he is in the process of being perfected. When a Christian sins, he is restored to spiritual fellowship upon his confession because of the eternal effectiveness of Christ's sacrifice (1 John 2:1–2). A Christian can be confident that he is in Christ when he is obediently keeping Christ's commandments and living in close fellowship with Him (1 John 2:3–6, John 15:10–14).

Are you and your present or future partner both Christians? Jesus said "I am the way, the truth, and the life; no man cometh unto the Father, but by me" (John 14:6). This means that there is only one way to come to God. Luke reiterates, "Neither is there salvation in any other: for there is none other name under heaven given among men, whereby we must be saved" (Acts 4:12). Jesus defines eternal life, saying, "And this is life eternal, that they might know thee the only true God, and Jesus Christ, whom thou hast sent" (John 17:3).

If you have any doubts about the salvation of your future partner, you would be wise to postpone the wedding ceremony until you are certain. Marriage is for life. Make sure you are both rightly related to God through His Son, Jesus Christ. If you are married, and either of you is uncertain if you are a Christian, speak with your minister or someone you believe is a Christian. God wants you to be sure of your salvation and not to be in doubt. God's purpose is clear! He said, "These things have I written...that ye may *know* that ye have eternal life..." (I John 5:13, emphasis mine).

1.   Describe how you became a Christian.

2. Explain how your future or present partner came to Christ.

3. What does 2 Corinthians 6:14 and 17 prohibit, and why is this important?

4. In Amos 3:3, we find the proverbial question, "Can two walk together, except they be agreed?" How does this question relate to marriage?

5. Solomon was wise in many areas, but he was unwise in his relationships with women. He loved what God forbade. Read 1 Kings 11 and cite three sins Solomon committed.

a. v. 1

b. vv. 1–3

c. v. 6

Marriage involves three: God, you, and your present or future partner. A triangle illustrates the relationships. You and your partner represent the left and right sides of the triangle. God is at the top. The closer you move up to God, the closer you will become to your partner.

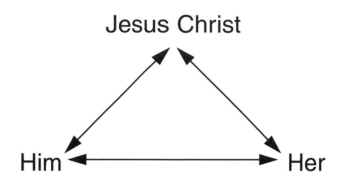

Some couples are estranged from one another because they are not close to God. They are negligent in their devotions and they sporadically read their Bibles. This coldness towards God also freezes up their spousal relationship. The warmth of their marital union becomes exposed, and their hearts turn to ice. Why does this occur? Because the further they are from God, the more they become self-centered and self-absorbed.

To reverse this coldness, God invites you to "Draw near to God and He will draw near to you" (James 4:8). If you seek to be closer to God, you will also become closer to your present or future partner!

List 3 things you will do to become closer to God.

1.

2.

3.

YOUR MOTIVATIONS

Both sexes share common motivations for marrying, but their order of importance might vary.

1. List below some of the reasons why men and women marry. The most common is "all my friends are getting married." Include others, both positive and negative.

Why women marry could include,

Why men marry could include,

2.   What reasons above are important to you and why?

3.   What reasons do you think are important to your partner and why?

Are you ready for marriage? From *Women Men Love/Women Men Leave,* Connell Cowan and Melvyn Kinder offer "10 Secrets Happy Couples Share." They state, "Marriage is not a cure-all. The rewards of marriage are so highly praised that people come to believe it is the antidote to salve old wounds from childhood or former loves. But marriage is not a solution to personal problems. No matter how close your marriage, you and your spouse are individuals before you are a couple."[7]

This observation is accurate. If a man struggles with self-control before he is married, marriage will not automatically make him into a self-disciplined and mature person. If a woman is enveloped in fears, she will not overcome them simply by getting married. God can work in his or her life, but it is not the marriage that makes the difference. A wiser person will wait and work on his personal problems before he assumes the responsibilities of married life.

GOD'S WORD

1. Read Genesis 2:18–25, giving special thought to 18, 23–24, and answer the following:

    A. Who said it was not good that man should be alone, and what did He do about it?

    B. What does "helper" or "help meet" mean?

    C. What is the meaning or significance of Adam's verbal response when God brought Eve to Adam (23)?

    D. What does verse 24 mean?

2. The book of Proverbs contains a collection of wise sayings about the whole of life.

    A. What does 18:22 say about the choice of a wife?

    B. What further insight may be gained from 19:14?

3. What specific instructions were given to man in Genesis 1:27–28 at the beginning of history regarding sex and children?

4. Ephesians 5:21–33 indicates how the marriage relationship is to reflect the spiritual relationship between Christ and the Church (His redeemed bride).

   A. What does verse 21 mean?

   B. How can the wife help her husband assume his position of leadership? See verses 22, 24 (i.e., support your husband's decisions, especially in front of the children).

   C. From verses 25 and 28, in what two ways are husbands commanded to love their wives?

   D. How can a husband abuse his position as head of the family? (i.e., becoming a tyrant or dictator in the home).

YOUR FOUNDATIONS

1. The value of a solid foundation of a house is taught in Matthew 7:24–27. Applying this to marriage, what needs to go into a solid foundation for marriage? List 3 biblical building blocks (i.e., couples must love God first and then one another intently).

2. A weak foundation for marriage can lead to destruction. List the 3 opposites of the 3 building blocks you cited above.

3. Read Psalm 11:3 and 1 Corinthians 3:10–15. Decide on what can undermine the foundations of marriage and list three examples (i.e., placing too much value on material possessions).

ACTION FOR LIVING

1. As you evaluate your relationship, discuss the things each of you appreciates about it and list 3 examples.

2. List those areas that need immediate improvement.

3. Choose one or more areas from the list above and write out what you plan to do in order to bring about change.

SUMMARY

Marriage is fulfilling, but it is also hard work. Successful Christian marriages are made up of two committed Christians who are growing in their relationship to God and in their intimacy with one another.

Look at the godly couples in your church. These examples are healthy believers who handle stress and disappointments according to God's Word. They are teachable because they are willing to listen to wise counsel, and they seek to practice what they believe.

Any exemplary couple is a submissive couple where both the husband and the wife submit to the Lordship of Jesus Christ. Neither one wants to "wear the pants" in the family because both are committed to following the servant-leader model that Jesus demonstrated. Last, but not least, the exemplary couple is realistic about their relationship. They do not demand perfection from one another, and they share realistic expectations about one another.

Pray with your partner often. Ask God to equip you to lay the spiritual foundations for an excellent marriage! If you are sincere, He will enable you.

Personal Reflections

Now that the premarital session or the Bible Study is over, reflect on what you have learned.

Love

Study Two

Songs are sung about it. Some have lived for it, and others have died for it. Apparently love is valuable and highly coveted. But just what is this thing called love?

Dr. Joyce Brothers was asked about love in her advice column entitled "I Love You: Know What I Mean?" A young woman writes, asking,

> Dear Dr. Brothers: My boyfriend constantly tells me that he loves me, but I'm never quite sure what that means. I guess what I'm wondering is: Does that phrase mean the same thing to him as it does to me? My girl-friend tells me that I should stop worrying and accept it at face value. She says that "I love you" means "I love you" and that's all there is to it.[8]

Does this sound like love to you? In the same newspaper, a young man writes to Ann Landers about the identical subject. In "Love – or its Kissing Cousin," he requests her to run a previous article that distinguishes love from infatuation. What is infatuation? Ann Landers writes,

> Infatuation is instant desire. It is one set of glands calling to another. Love is friendship that has caught fire. It takes root and grows – one day at a time. Infatuation is marked by a feeling of insecurity. You are excited and eager, but not genuinely happy. There are nagging doubts, unanswered questions, little bits and pieces about your beloved that you would as soon not examine too closely. It might spoil the dream. Love is the quiet understanding and the mature acceptance of imperfection. It is real. It gives you strength and grows beyond you, to bolster your beloved. You are warmed by his presence, even when he is away. Miles do not separate you. You want him nearer. But near or far, you know he

13

is yours and you can wait. Infatuation says, "We must get married right away. I can't risk losing him." Love says, "Be patient. Don't panic. Plan your future with confidence." Infatuation has an element of sexual excitement. If you are honest, you will admit it is difficult to be in one another's company unless you are sure it will end in intimacy. Love is the maturation of friendship. You must be friends before you can be lovers. Infatuation lacks confidence. When he's away, you wonder if he's cheating. Sometimes you check. Love means trust. You are calm, secure, and unthreatened. He feels that trust, and it makes him even more trustworthy. Infatuation may lead you to do things that you will regret later, but love never does.[9]

Although a secular columnist, Landers is correct about infatuation. It is a cheap copy of the real thing. Like a bootleg copy of an original video, infatuation is a poor imitation of love.

LOVE DEFINED

What does God say about love? The New Testament was written in Koine (common) Greek, and there are several Greek words used for love. While some of these words overlap in their usage, each one represents a distinct meaning.

The common word for love is *phileo*, and means "love, have affection for, like."[10] While it is used for God's love for man, it is mostly used for humans love to one another. For example, its root word is combined with other words to form compound words used of wives loving their husbands, love for an immediate family member, and love for one's children (Titus 2:4).

Another word for love is *agape*. This word is used to describe the love that the Father has for the Son. In John 17:26, it says, "And I have declared unto them thy name, and will declare it: that the love wherewith thou hast loved me may be in them, and I in them." The love the Father has for the Son is the strongest and purest love. This type of love is also used to describe God's love for unrepentant sinners. The Bible teaches, "But God commendeth his love toward us, in that, while we were yet sinners, Christ died for us" (Romans 5:8). This unconditional love of Christ is the genuine love described by the term agape. Further, the Christians who worshipped in Ephesus loved other Christians with the unadulterated, or *agape* love as well (Ephesians 1:15).

Since there is an overlap in the usage of the words in the New Testament, it is incorrect to say that *agape* love is God's love and *phileto* love is human love. But how can we distinguish them? *Agape* love is a stronger love, and *phileo* is a weaker love. Your goal must be to love God, your partner, and your neighbor with the strongest love. Therefore, Christians need to imitate the *agape* love that the Father has for the Son and that the Ephesian Christians had for God and for other believers.

The third word for love is *eros*, and means "passionate love."[11] This Greek word is not used in the Greek New Testament.

GOD ILLUSTRATES PERFECT LOVE

The Bible teaches that God loves you with the strongest and purest love. Consider how God's love is demonstrated in the following passages.

1. How is love illustrated in John 3:16?

2. What does love do in this verse?

3. In what way is Romans 5:8 an example of God's love?

LOVE DESCRIBED

God has not left us to guess what love is. He provides Christians with a detailed description of love in 1 Corinthians 13:4–8. Under each description, write out the meaning and an example of how you do, or will apply it.

1. Love suffers long (v. 4).
    Meaning: For example: love is long-tempered or patient.
    My Application: "I will not finish the sentence of my partner. Instead, I will wait patiently, even when she speaks too slowly and I already know what she is going to say."

2. Love is kind (v. 4). See also Ephesians 4:32.
    Meaning:

    My Application:

3. Love envies not (v. 4). See also Galatians 5:26.
    Meaning:

    My Application:

4. Love does not vaunt itself, is not puffed up or prideful (v. 4). See also 2 Timothy 3:1–2, 1 Corinthians 4:6, 18–19.

Meaning:

My Application:

5. Love does not behave itself unseemingly nor is it rude (v. 5). See also Philippians 4:8–9.
    Meaning:

    My Application:

6. Love seeks not its own (v. 5) nor is it self-seeking. See also Philippians 2:3–5.
    Meaning:

    My Application:

7. Love is not easily provoked or angered (v. 5). See also Ephesians 4:1–3.
    Meaning:

    My Application:

8. Love thinks no evil nor does it keep written records of others' sins (v. 5). See also Romans 12:9 and Philippians 4:8.
Meaning:

My Application:

9. Love rejoices not in iniquity, but in truth (v. 6)
Meaning:

My Application:

A. To best understand what rejoicing in truth means, define truth. What or who is truth according to these passages?

1. John 14:6

2. John 17:17

3. 1 Timothy 3:15

4. 1 John 5:6

B. How should this effect the way you live?

10. Love bears all things (v. 7).
    Meaning:

    Application:

11. Love believes all things (v. 7).
    Meaning:

    Application:

12. Love hopes all things (v. 7). See also Hebrews 6:17–20.
    Meaning:

    Application:

13. Love endures all things (v. 7). Remember your vows?
    Meaning:

    Application:

14. Love never fails (v. 8). Remember Proverbs 10:12, which says, "Hatred stirreth up strife, but love covereth all sins." See also Ephesians 3:17–19.
    Meaning:

Application:

This may sound impossible to do everyday, but remember God's Word, which guarantees that you can do anything God wants you to do because He will provide the strength and the resources!

SUMMARY

Agape love gives and sacrifices without ulterior motives. It unselfishly reaches out and patiently aims to achieve what is best for someone else. Biblical love is the highest priority, and the Christian life must radiate the love of Christ. This love is not the same as what the world calls love. Unbelievers define love in a variety of ways, but they all have one thing in common: their definitions are all wrong. For example, baby boomers might remember a popular movie from the 70's which erroneously redefined love. The title of the movie was "Love Story," and a reoccurring theme was "Love is Never Having to Say You're Sorry." The movie made millions of dollars, but its message was false. Love is not, "never having to say you're sorry." Other unbeliever's definitions equate love with sexual desire, or ecstatic feelings. They confuse pseudo or artificial love with real love.

Love seeks the other person's interests ahead of its own. Love is selfless and aims to build up. Love is a verb as well as a noun. It's action oriented and is never static. Love perseveres and does not initiate divorce proceedings (citing irreconcilable differences). *Agape* love works hard to make relationships work as God intended.

A Christian poster pictured a dejected football player sitting with his head between his legs. In huge letters, it read, "I QUIT!" At the bottom in tiny letters it read, "I didn't"; and it was signed *Jesus Christ*. This is the kind of love that honors God and brings Him glory! In your marriage, this is the type of love you and your partner must aim to develop. It won't happen overnight, but it will materialize if you work on making it work!

Pray together and ask God to teach you how to practice His unselfish, agape love. When you are unloving, confess it to God and start loving!

Personal Reflections

Now that the premarital session or the Bible Study is over, reflect on what you have learned.

Perception and Sensitivity

Study Three

In study two, you learned about *agape* love. In this study you will explore the perversion of self-love, right and wrong platforms for your self-image, the pitfalls of wrongly evaluating others, and the importance of being sensitive to others.

SELF-LOVE

The Bible warns about people who love themselves. They are self-absorbed and self-centered. In their world, only one really matters. They live to please themselves.

In 2 Timothy 3:1–2, God said through Paul, "...in the last days...men shall be lovers of their own selves." The Greek word for "lovers of their own selves" is *philautos* (*phileo*, or love + *autos*, or self), which means "loving self."[12] Self-love can destroy any marriage because it is the opposite of agape love. *Agape* love is empty of self, while the *philautos* type of love is full of self because it is the love of self.

In Matthew 22:35–40, an expert in the Jewish Law was testing Jesus. He asked "...which is the greatest commandment in the law?" (v. 36). The Law of Moses contained Ten Commandments, but the laws of Judaism had grown to 619. Of these, 254 were positive and 365 were negative laws.

1. From this test question, Jesus explains two spiritual priorities. List them.

2. According to verse 39, what is implied by the phrase "...love thy neighbor as thyself?"

Nowhere in Scripture are you told to love yourself, since you already love yourself and take care of yourself. God commands you to love Him and to love your neighbor as you already love yourself!

3. Read Luke 10:25–37.

    A. Who are you commanded to love?

    B. Who is your neighbor?

Explaining this passage, John Piper says,

> Jesus is saying to the lawyer: Take note how much you love yourself, how you try to get the best place in the synagogues, how you seek to be seen praying on the streets, how you exercise all rigor to maintain purity. Now my commandment to you is: Take all that zeal, all that ingenuity, all that perseverance, and with it, seek your neighbor's well-being. And with that Jesus cuts the nerve of every merely selfish lifestyle. All our in-born self-seeking is made the measure of our self-giving. Do we seek to satisfy our hunger? Then we must with a similar urgency feed our hungry neighbor. Do we long for advancement in the company? Then we must seek out ways to give others as much opportunity and to stir up their will to achieve. Do we love to make A's on tests? Then we must tutor the poor student who would love it no less. Do we hate to be laughed at and mocked? Then let there never be found on our lips a mocking word.[13]

Being in love with oneself is sinful. God calls you to redirect that love to Him and to your neighbor.

SELF-IMAGE: PSYCHOLOGICAL VIEW

Modern psychology worships the concept of the self-image. For them, the greatest need is for people to feel good about themselves. Christian psychologist Chris Thurman exposes the idolatrous approach of Matthew McKay and Patrick Fanning by quoting their book, *Self-Esteem*, which states,

- I am worthwhile because I breathe and feel and am aware
- I am basically all right as I am
- It's all right to meet my needs as I see fit
- Everything I do is an attempt to meet legitimate needs
- My basic job in life is explaining my awareness
- Today you like yourself more than yesterday, and tomorrow you will like yourself more than today

These six statements represent the foundation upon which the god of secular psychology is mounted. Thurman then asks,

> Have you ever heard more self-serving, narcissistic hogwash in your whole life?[14]

Thurman is correct that these statements are narcissistic hogwash since they deny the basic teachings of the Bible, and they worship the god of self. For example, the second affirmation says, "I am basically alright as I am." God's Word says the opposite. In Romans 3:9–20, Scripture teaches that all human beings are sinful. Psychology has disregarded God and His Word and is attempting to replace His truth with its own false value system.

Christians need to separate truth from modern psychology and empty philosophy. Christian bookstores are full of self-help books that are primarily secular, but have a handful of Scriptures sprinkled throughout. These books are dangerous and must be avoided. British theologian J. I. Packer warns,

> ...modern Christians... spread a thin layer of Bible teaching over the mixture of popular psychology..., but their overall approach clearly reflects the narcissism – the "selfism" or "meism"... that is the way of the world.[15]

Packer's words are wise. The attempt to integrate truth and error has caught many off guard, and many more do not see the subtle differences between secular psychological principles and the Word of God. Christians must exercise more spiritual discernment. What does the Bible teach about self-image?

SELF-IMAGE: BIBLICAL VIEW

1. The Bible is a spiritual mirror that enables you to accurately see yourself as God sees you. Before you became a Christian, what did you look like according to Eph. 2:1–10?

   A. Your non-Christian past (vv. 1–3). What six phrases described you?
      Example: Dead in trespasses and sins (v. 1)

   B. Your present position (vv. 4–10). What four phrases describe you?
      Example: "Quickened," or made spiritually alive (v. 5)

A biblical self-image is neither a good self-image, nor a bad self-image. It is an accurate self-image in which believers grasp that they were "children of wrath" (v. 3) and that they became, through faith in Jesus Christ (v. 8), "his workmanship" (v. 10).

The psychological model is like plastic – it's man-made. It is not genuine. The biblical model of one's self-image is right because God is its author. He described who Christians are and how they should feel about themselves and the world.

2. Do you follow the psychological model or the biblical model on self-image? Explain which you've chosen and why?

3. How can self-worth or self-image be wrongly measured according to 2 Corinthians 10:12?

4. Write out what these verses teach about how God sees you.

    A. John 3:16

    B. 1 Peter 5:7

C. Jeremiah 31:3

D. John 15:9

5. You were created in the image and likeness of God. But because Adam and Eve sinned, you became a sinner too. As a sinner, God must forgive you through personal faith in His Son. After you're converted, you're progressively transformed into the likeness of Jesus Christ.

   A. In Genesis 1:27, how did God originally create you?

   B. That image was damaged. According to Romans 5:12, what happened?

   C. How is God restoring the severed fellowship according to Colossians 1:15–22?

D. Christians are being recreated in Christ. This is a lifelong process that begins when you are rightly related to God through His Son Jesus Christ and ends when you are with Him in heaven. Write out what these verses say about this sanctifying process.

1. 2 Corinthians 3:18

2. Colossians 3:10

3. 2 Peter 1:4

4. 1 John 3:2–3

EVALUATING OTHERS

Christians occasionally judge others based only on what they can see. List seven wrong standards some use to judge other people.

1 Samuel 16:7

1. Example: Judging someone based upon his or her physical appearance.

2.

Matthew 13:55–56

3.

John 1:45–46

4.

Jeremiah 9:23–24

5.

6.

7.

Christians need to see themselves as God does and learn how to view others as God views them.

SENSITIVITY TOWARDS OTHERS

1. Sensitivity is directly related to what you think about. List eight descriptions from Philippians 4:8 on the content of a God-honoring thought life. Think about things that are, for example, true.

Some diet programs state that you are what you eat. The Bible teaches you are what you think! That is why your thought life is so important.

2. Give three examples of how you are applying Philippians 4:8.

3. How can 2 Corinthians 10:5 help?

4. What does God command in 1 Peter 1:13?

5. According to Proverbs 16:3, How can you be a partner with God in controlling your thoughts?

It is important that you remember that "As a man thinketh in his heart, so is he" (Proverbs 23:7). This means that your thought life is central to the attitudes you develop. If you think unwholesome thoughts, then you will develop unwholesome attitudes towards the opposite sex, and your attitude problem could lead to unwholesome activities. Guard your minds and discipline your thought life. Remember, trash in, trash out!

6. Sensitivity to others is directly related to your attitudes. Identify the God-honoring attitudes in the following passages.

Philippians 3:13–14

Example: Having humility and not being an authority on everything.

Romans 14:10–13

James 5:16

SUMMARY

The world is not short on love. The problem is that it is misdirected, and it is the wrong type of love. Instead of loving God and loving one's neighbor, people love themselves. This self-love is idolatrous because it is a worship of self. Psychology has attempted to normalize self-love, and many Christian psychologists have bought into it. Christians from many denominations have swallowed this distortion, and many fail to see the sinfulness of bowing to the god of self.

Psychology has heralded the self-esteem, self-worth, and self-image concepts so effectively that many Christians believe that these are biblical teachings. Sadly, the Bride of Christ is flirting with man-made, psychological theories. Christians must return to the Bible for guidance and stop listening to the wisdom of this world.

How does all of this relate to marriage? First, if you are in love with yourself, you will not be able to love your wife as "...Christ also loved the Church, and gave himself for it..." (Ephesians 5:25). Second, if your affection and devotion are directed inwardly, you will not "...love the Lord thy God with all thy heart, and with all thy soul, and with all thy mind, and with all thy strength..." (Mark 12:30). You must flee from self-love like Joseph fled from Potiphar's sensual wife (Genesis 39:12). Third, if you are focusing on your own self-image, you are ignoring God. The Bible teaches that you need to be "Looking unto Jesus the author and finisher of our faith...lest ye be wearied and faint in your minds" (Hebrews 12:2–3). This means you must stop thinking only about yourself and loving yourself and refocus upon Christ and love Him! Remember the diagram on page 5 that illustrated how you will be increasingly closer to your partner as you become closer to Jesus Christ.

A Christian's marriage can only succeed when both partners are in love with God first, and then with one another. Every spouse must guard against becoming overly judgmental and must exercise genuine humility. This means Christians must control their thoughts and feelings so they will not respond to one another according to the flesh. Proper attitudes and dependence upon God are necessary for marriages to grow into spiritually healthy unions.

Friend, adjust your attitudes and depend on God. If you do, you will grow! Pray for and with your partner so you both will grow in sensitivity toward one another.

Personal Reflections

Now that the premarital session or the Bible Study is over, reflect on what you have learned.

Communication

Study Four

How well do you communicate? To some, communication comes naturally. To others, just thinking about communication causes them to break out in cold sweats. *Reader's Digest* offers,

> As a friend and I rode to town in her car, I noticed she had a radar detector mounted on the dashboard. "Gladys," I asked, "why do you have a Fuzzbuster?" "For my birthday, I asked my husband for a Dustbuster," she replied. "This is what I got."[16]

The sad truth is this kind of miscommunication is commonplace in many marriages. The author has been in the ministry for over 25 years, and he has discovered that the number one problem in most marriages is the couple's failure to communicate as God commands.

God has not left you to guess how to communicate biblically. He has graciously provided principles that can equip you to be a better communicator.

GOD'S PRINCIPLES ON
GOOD AND POOR COMMUNICATION
FROM PROVERBS

Proverbs is packed with practical wisdom on how and how not to communicate. The following passages provide several types of words that should be used and many that must be avoided.

1. **Poor communication** is evident in these passages. All of them indicate doing something in excess. For positive statements, think about its opposite.

    A. 10:19 – too much

    B. 15:1; 13:3 –

    C. 18:13 –

    D. 12:18 –

E. 16:32 –

F. 11:13; 16:28; 17:9; 18:8 –

G. 18:6–7 – _____ words

2. **Good communication** is exemplified in these passages. Describe the type of "good" words. Note that the opposite may be asked for.

A. 12:25; 16:24 – Example: Wholesome words

B. 15:2; 16:23; 20:15 –

C. 18:23; 25:15 –

D. 25:9 –

E. 25:11 –

F. 29:11 –

G. 31:26; Eph. 4:32 –

BARRIERS TO COMMUNICATION

Communication can be thwarted and corrupted, creating barriers that block effective communication. Holly Phillips, answering an interviewer's questions in a devotional entitled *How Can Men and Women Connect?*, candidly tells about the poor communication in her marriage. She states,

> I struggled for three years before I finally decided to deal with anger and frustration…When our needs aren't met, women tend to wait until we're so stinking frustrated that we blow up.[17]

Phillips speaks about her needs. Couples need to be careful when speaking about their needs. It is easy to fall into the "needs theology" trap in which couples perceive life through the fulfillment or lack of fulfillment of their needs. To keep a biblical perspective on needs, remember the patience of Job. He was in the center of God's will while he was suffering, but his needs were unmet for a period of time. This means that you may be in the center of God's will and still experience depravation in some areas of your life.

Obviously, huge walls had surrounded the Phillips' marital communication. Thankfully, Holly dealt with her intense anger and frustration. As a result, her marital relationship improved dramatically as well as her communication.

What other barriers might thwart communication? Another common barrier to marital communication is a devaluation of differences. Some might think that their differences are unimportant, and this may signal that there is an additional problem. In "Why Husbands Won't Talk" (condensed from *Love is Never Enough)*, Aaron T. Beck (M.D.) states,

> When ironing out conflicts, many women feel, *The marriage is working as long as we can talk about it.* Husbands think, *The relationship is not working if we have to keep talking about it.*[18]

Men and women do not always understand communication identically. They each need to learn how their own partners communicate and what they mean by what they say.

Marriage is made up of many important parts, but couples must learn to appreciate and prioritize communication in their marriages. If they do, their rate of success will increase. Successfully married couples are men and women who practice biblically based, healthy, wholesome, and character building communication skills. This takes time and work, but it's worth it.

Don't communicate like the couple that sits at the breakfast table, and the husband speaks from behind his newspaper and says, "What do you mean I never communicate? Don't you read your e-mail?"

IDENTIFYING THE BARRIERS TO COMMUNICATION FROM PROVERBS

Look up each verse in your Bible and write out the barriers you discern from each passage.

A. Proverbs 11:12 – Example: Speaking when you should be quiet. The real art of communication is not only to say the right thing at the right time, but also to leave unsaid the wrong thing at the tempting moment.

B. Proverbs 12:16

C. Proverbs 12:22

D. Proverbs 21:19

E. Proverbs 29:20

Disagreements in marriage are to be expected. They happen because we are still in the process of becoming like our Lord. No one is perfect. Therefore, anticipate some friction and be prepared to handle it in a way that does not compromise your testimony for Christ. Remember that it is acceptable to disagree, as long as you disagree agreeably and so long as you solve problems biblically!

THE RELATIONSHIP BETWEEN
YOUR WITNESS AND YOUR COMMUNICATION

Every time you communicate, you are testifying for or against Christ. This is because people hear your words and sense your attitude by the language you use and the way you express yourself. Your words, phrases, volume, and speed all contribute to the message you are communicating and the witness you are portraying. Based on Ephesians 4:1–6, Jeffery S. Forrey wrote,

> When I communicate, I must be concerned about setting a good example of Christ to others (v. 1), being humble (v. 2), gentle (v. 2), patient, bearing with one another (v. 2), and be concerned about harmony in the Church (vv. 3–6).[19]

This is the conscientious outlook that exalts God. The way you speak does effect the impact of your words. I challenge you to adopt a similar strategy in your witness to the non-believing world and in your communication among God's people. If you do, God will be honored!

GOD'S PRINCIPLES ON COMMUNICATION
FROM THE NEW TESTAMENT

A brief tour through the New Testament yields principles on the type of words you should use and the categories of words you must avoid. Identify the type of words you should use.

1. Matthew 5:37 – Example: Concise and clear
This verse was illustrated in a cartoon showing three men speaking to their pastor, saying, "Let your yea be yea, your nay be nay, and your 'in conclusion' be your conclusion."

2. Luke 4:22

3. John 6:68

4. Acts 26:25

5. Ephesians 4:15

6. Ephesians 4:29b

7. Ephesians 6:20

8. 1 Thessalonians 4:18

9. 1 Timothy 6:3

10. 2 Timothy 1:13

11. Revelation 21:5

Identify the category of words that you must avoid.

1. Acts 6:11 – Example: Blasphemous words that deny God or His Word.

2. Acts 6:13 – Example: False or lying words.

3. Acts 15:24

4. Romans 16:18

5. 2 Corinthians 4:2

6. Ephesians 4:25a

7. Ephesians 4:29a

8. Ephesians 4:31

9. Ephesians 5:5, 2 Peter 2:18

10. Colossians 3:8

11. 1 Thessalonians 2:5

12. 1 Timothy 6:4

13. 3 John 1:10

14. Jude 16

From these passages it is clear that there are types of words that you may use, and there are others that you need to eliminate from your vocabulary.

In Ephesians 4:22–24, Paul uses the "put off" and "put on" metaphor to illustrate the Christian life. Believers must put off their carnal ways and put on the new man, in Christ. The new man is the new person God made you into when you were converted to Jesus Christ. List below four examples of how you will apply these verses to communication. Include two ways you will put off and two ways you will put on, or practice, these principles.

Example: I'm going to think more before I speak so I'll be able to have more control over what I say. Speaking more slowly will also help me to have a better attitude when I speak.

SUMMARY

The communication process is complex but must be prioritized by every couple. While men baby their cars and women care about their clothes, couples frequently allow their communication to wane. Christian couples must reverse this trend and work hard at achieving the God-honoring communication described in the Bible.

The barriers to communication in your marriage need to be leveled one at a time. These could include the failure to deal with one's sin, the maintaining of a cavalier attitude about communication, anger and deceit, discontentment and impetuousness, and speaking when you ought to listen.

Christian couples need to grasp the link between their witness and the way in which they communicate. It is fruitless to give a stirring testimony, but then contradict what you said by your failure to biblically communicate with your partner. Non-believers need to see your testimony in everyday life, as well as hear it.

Your vocabulary and way in which you communicate those words must be aligned with the Word of God. Some have said it doesn't matter what you say as long as the other person knows how you feel about them. This common expression is false. It does matter what you say, and it certainly does make a difference how you say it. Christians need to wake up to the realization that communication is central in the Christian life, and Christ will judge every believer on how they have communicated. This inevitable judgment (2 Cor. 5:10; 1 Peter 5:4; 1 John 2:28; 3:2) should motivate you to work on and improve your communication. God reminds us that "…not he that commendeth himself is approved, but whom the Lord commendeth" (2 Cor. 10:18).

Pray with your partner and ask God to equip you to speak as He desires! God is an expert on communication. He can help!

Personal Reflections

Now that the premarital session or the Bible Study is over, reflect on what you have learned.

Consideration: Selflessness or Selfishness in Marriage

Study Five

In Christian marriage, one plus one equals one. This means that you must voluntarily sacrifice your individuality in order to form a partnership. In Christian marriage, "mine" and "yours" becomes "ours." Friction occurs when one partner hoards more of his or her share of the resources. Conflict also arises when one attempts to dominate or control the other. This is simply immature selfishness. Therefore, you need to learn to be considerate of one another.

What does God teach in the following verses relating to consideration and unselfishness, and how should you apply them? Your responses should be tailored to your relationship with your present or future partner.

1. Philippians 2:3–4

   • "in lowliness of mind"

   • "let each esteem others better"

   • "Look…on the things of others"

2. Colossians 3:19

3. 1 Peter 3:7
    - "giving honor unto the wife"

4. Romans 12:10
    - "in honor preferring one another"

5. I Samuel 1:4–8

6. Luke 6:27–31
    - "Love your enemies" v. 27

    - "Bless…pray for them who…use you" v. 28

    - "offer also the other" v. 29

    - "Give to every man" v. 30

    - And as you would…do…to them" v. 31

God's will is for believers to be humble and unselfish. When Christians are not prideful, they'll find that it is easier to be considerate of one another. But be careful and guard your heart because pride suffocates humility.

CONSIDERATION OBSERVED IN OTHERS

1. Cite two examples of consideration you have observed in others. This could include your parents, in-laws, or other couples at church.

2. Ask two Christian couples, who you consider to be considerate, what "the secret" is to showing consideration to one another. Record their answers here.

CONSIDERATION APPLIED

1. Read Ephesians 4:1–3.

   A. From the list below, check the actions you think apply; then write out how you are applying it or will apply it. If a statement does not apply, explain why it is wrong.

   ❒ I must admit my error when I am wrong.

❒ I should wait for my partner to admit his/her error first.

❒ God wants me to look for ways to help my partner.

❒ I am always allowed to stand up for my rights.

❒ I need to consider timing before making requests or sharing discouraging news with my partner.

B. The Bible teaches Christians are to be "forbearing one another in love" (Ephesians 4:2). This means believers are to be patient with each another. Provide an example of how you have applied this truth in the past and one of how you will apply it in the future.

- Past –

- Future –

CONSIDERATION UNDER PRESSURE

It is easier to show consideration when life is uncomplicated and you have few problems. It is another story when you are stressed out, overweight, unemployed, or facing a personal illness or tragedy in life. Life is not easy, and marriage is not the answer to all of your needs or problems. Marriage is difficult and necessitates diligence and a willingness to work at it.

In John 8, Jesus was under pressure, and His enemies were attempting to entrap Him. Put in a seemingly lose-lose situation, it appeared that nothing He could choose would be right. If He consented to have the woman stoned, He would have been accused of lacking compassion. If He had agreed to let her go, He would have had the proverbial finger stuck in His face for violating the Mosaic Law which mandated death for adultery. Thus, He was outwardly trapped. As the God-man, fully God and fully man, Jesus could have condemned the woman for her wickedness. But Jesus responded differently. Meditate on John 8:1–11 and imagine yourself as each of the main characters in the account.

1. What did you learn from John 8:1–11?

- About the woman who committed adultery?
  Example: Although the woman was invariably ashamed, she did not deny her sin, nor did she attempt to rationalize or cover it up. Therefore, when I sin, I should not attempt to gloss over it or cover it up. I must honestly confess it to God.

- About the religious leaders called Scribes and Pharisees?

- About Jesus? Cite at least three observations.
  Example: Jesus was merciful. He did not give her what she deserved, but He did give her what she did not deserve.

2. Provide two examples that illustrate what you need to change in your life. Consider the observations you wrote about Jesus in the John 8 confrontation.

SUMMARY

In America, couples are considerate at least once a year. This "Day of Consideration" occurs in February. Hallmark prints millions of cards for men and women to buy, and flower shops are busier than WalMart on Christmas Eve.

Valentine's Day is the day when men and women think about each other and buy cards, candy, flowers, or clothes to show that unique person how special he or she is. In February, worldly consideration is everywhere. But consideration is much more than this annual gift giving. Consideration is unselfishness. Husbands and wives need to practice consideration everyday of the year. The thoughtfulness and sensitivity shown on Valentine's Day must saturate the couple's relationship all year long.

Consideration is thinking of your partner before you focus upon yourself. Considerate partners are not demanding, but help one another. Husbands willingly honor their wives, and wives genuinely respect their husbands. They practice mutual forbearance and avoid debate over every issue.

The golden rule, "And as ye would that men should do to you, do ye also to them" (Luke 6:31), is the guiding principle of the day. This is evidenced by the couple's mutual accountability before God and each before the other. When marital friction threatens their companionship, both take the initiative to seek and grant forgiveness.

A considerate partner does not stand on his or her individual "rights," but instead, voluntarily lays those "rights" at Christ's feet and serves Him by serving his or her spouse! A considerate husband willingly gives up a golf game, or whatever is important to him, so his wife may participate in Christian Women's Retreats, go shopping, or have lunch with a friend. An unselfish wife gladly adjusts her schedules so her husband may participate in Christian Men's Retreats, occasionally hunt, fish, or do whatever is vital to him. The motivation for husbands and wives must be the desire to be considerate and to demonstrate it by one's actions.

The key to the lock is self-sacrifice. Measuring how far you are willing to go or gauging how much you are willing to do for your partner will reveal how considerate or inconsiderate you really are towards him or her. Christians, be considerate! Rightly motivated consideration honors God and it will deepen your relationship with your partner.

Personal Reflections

Now that the premarital session or the Bible Study is over, reflect on what you have learned.

Marital Sexuality

Study Six

The non-Christian world has distorted sexuality and cheapened it. The world's acceptance of evolution is one reason for this. If humans descended from animals, and humans are nothing more than animals, then rules and regulations about sexuality are unnecessary. Sex for animals is simply a mating ritual. But God's Word plainly states that humans were created in the image and likeness of God. This means that human beings are not animals, but God's special creation.

God provided standards to regulate the sexuality of His image bearers. This means that the purpose and practice of sexuality was determined and created by God. Since God created sex, it is not dirty or despicable. Human sexuality is a divine gift, and it is a holy activity when it is practiced between a Christian husband and wife! Some Christians misunderstand God's Word and mistakenly believe that sex is only a necessity, and that it should not be enjoyed. People with this perspective are misinformed and need to study what God said about sexuality in His Holy Bible.

Sexuality is not a taboo subject, but one that must be understood within the parameters that God has defined in the Holy Bible. This study will focus upon three areas of sexuality. First, God's purpose of sexuality will be uncovered. Second, where and between whom is God's plan for sexuality to occur will be addressed. Finally, we will search the Scriptures to discover the practice of marital sexuality.

THE THREE PURPOSES OF MARITAL SEXUALITY

1. The Purpose of marital sexuality is to expand physical families.

   A. What did God command Adam and Eve to do in Genesis 1:27–28?

   B. According to Genesis 4:1, how did Adam and Eve respond?

C. What is the relationship between 4:1 and 1:27–28?

D. How does Genesis 1:27–28 relate to you and your partner?

2. The purpose of marital sexuality is to expand the emotional and spiritual unity within the marriage relationship.

A. In Matthew 19:4–6, Jesus quotes Genesis 1:27 and 2:24. In what ways does the physical oneness contribute to emotional and spiritual oneness?

B. In Genesis 2:25, it says that both Adam and Eve were naked and unashamed. This nakedness related to not only their physical relationship, but also to the openness and transparency in their relationship.

- How comfortable are you with your own body?

- How comfortable are you with your partner's body?

- Rate your openness and transparency with your partner on a scale of 1 to 10, with 1 being the least. What blocks further openness and transparency?

- What can you do to improve your non-physical intimacy?

3. The Purpose of Marital Sexuality is to Enjoy Your Partner

   A. Proverbs 5:15–20

   In the Old Testament, one way that drinking water was gathered was by catching and saving the fresh rainwater. The Jews dug huge multi-leveled cisterns, which effectively collected and held the pure water. These cisterns were like mini reservoirs, and on some occasions, underground shafts supplied the liquid-life to the nearby villages and cities. Wells were also used, and these were deep holes that were dug to access the water from the subterranean level.

   In Proverbs 5:15–20, cisterns are used figuratively for something other than a system to catch the rain. This passage employs cisterns as a marital analogy.

   1. Within marriage, whom does "own cistern" and "own well" refer to (v. 15)?

   2. Fountains are used as another marital analogy. What does the "fountains" refer to, and in what ways are these "fountains" to be regulated (vv. 16–18a)?

   3. The context of Proverbs 5:15–20 is marital sexuality. What does "rejoice with the wife of thy youth" mean (v. 18b)?

   4. Explain "Let her be as the loving hind and pleasant roe (a "roe" or a "hind" is a deer); let her breasts satisfy thee at all

times; and be thou ravished always with her love" (v. 19).

5. Who does the "strange woman" or "stranger" in verse 20 represent, and what is prohibited?

6. Write three truths concerning man's relationship to God that are evident from verses 21–23.
   Example: God sees and knows what you are doing (v. 21).

B. In Song of Solomon 4:1–5 and 7:1–10, the conversation between married lovers is recorded. The author neither allegorizes this passage nor believes that it pictures Christ and the Church. Instead, the descriptions point to the physical bodies of married lovers and the pleasure that they are designed to enjoy. Write out what the body is compared with and how that comparison is significant. There is no need to be embarrassed here because God created every part of you, and it is holy when it is used as God intended. A Study Bible or a Bible commentary may be helpful.

SONG OF SOLOMON 7:1–10

To help you get started, some examples are given below. Now
you fill in the remainder.

Physical Body	Compared To	Significance
1. feet thighs	 precious jewels	 very valuable
2. navel belly		
3. two breasts	young, twin deer	tender, unspoiled beauty
4. neck eyes nose	tower of ivory	slender, imposing, and captivating
5. head hair		
6. statue breasts	palm tree cluster of grapes	stable & strong due to its deep root system luscious, ripe
7. smell	apples	sweetness and health
8. mouth	the best wine	celebration and highest delight

From these descriptions, what is God's message about marital sexuality?

C. Verse 10 reads, "I am my beloved's, and his desire is toward me." What does this mean?

- Is sexual desirableness wrong? Why or why not?

- What can you do to become more desirable to your partner?

- Why is this important?

- When will you do it?

THE PLACE OF MARITAL SEXUALITY

Study Hebrews 13:4, which states, "Marriage is honorable in all, and the bed undefiled: but whoremongers and adulterers God will judge." Write out your insights on the following phrases.

1. "Marriage is honorable in all..." (v. 4a).
The original Greek word for "honorable" means "held in honor, respected, valuable, precious." This same word is used in 1 Peter 1:19 as an adjective, describing the blood of Christ.

2. "...and the bed undefiled" (v. 4b).
"Undefiled" means "pure, in religious and moral sense." This same word is used to describe Jesus Christ in Hebrews 7:26.

3. "...but whoremongers and adulterers..." (v. 4c).
The original Greek word for "whoremongers" is a word from which the English word "pornography" is derived. The word transliterated is *pornos*, and means "one who practices sexual immorality." An adulterer is one who has broken his marriage covenant and is unfaithful to his marriage partner.

4. "...God will judge" (v. 4d).
The Greek word is in the future tense, which means that this verse

is pointing to the future judgment of mankind. Consider the following passages and then write your responses:
Acts 10:42; 17:31; Romans 2:16.

THE PRACTICE OF MARITAL SEXUALITY

The practice of marital sexuality will focus upon two passages of Scripture that provide numerous principles. These sections are 1 Corinthians 7:1–5 and Philippians 2:3.

1 Corinthians 7:1–5

Study 1 Corinthians 7:1–5 and express why you believe the following points are true or false.

1. I may participate in sex only when I feel like it.

2. Marital intimacy should be continuous and neither partner should, barring illness or mutual consent, withhold himself or herself from his or her partner (vv. 3–4).

3. It is selfish to withhold physical intimacy from my spouse (v. 5a).

4. It is acceptable to suspend sex for long periods of time.

5. When physical intimacy is interrupted, the abstinence may lead to satanic temptation (v. 5b).

Philippians 2:3

The Bible stresses the importance of putting others ahead of yourself. In Philippians 2:3 it says, "Let nothing be done through strife or vainglory, but in lowliness of mind let each esteem others better than themselves." Write your personal convictions below each statement.

1. Sexual intercourse should be *mutually enjoyable*. This means that any activity that one partner dislikes or is uncomfortable with should be avoided.

2. Sex should never be coerced or forced. This means that physical intimacy must be *mutually desired*.

3. Communicate what you like and dislike, without embarrassment. Your partner wants to know what you enjoy and what you desire. Therefore, show and tell him or her. You need to be *mutually active.*

4. God expects Christians to please their partners before they please themselves. You must be *mutually unselfish.*

SUMMARY

God's purpose for marital sexuality is to expand families, build unity within the marital relationship, and to be enjoyable. Sex in marriage is a wholesome activity and should be enjoyed often, without guilt or embarrassment. The primary goal of each partner must be to bring the other to maximum sexual fulfillment. Everything you do must be *mutually enjoyable* and *mutually desirable.* This is because your partner's body belongs to you, and your body belongs to your marital partner. There is no reason to be shy or intimidated. Sex between two committed marriage partners requires *mutual activity* and *mutual unselfishness.* Both spouses should be actively pursuing the other, but with unhurried and sensitive tenderness.

God's creation of the physical body is perfect, and His design is flawless. The physical body is an awesome and remarkable masterpiece. Human sexuality is God's gift for your good and His glory. Do not be ashamed or uncomfortable. God isn't, and He does not want you to be either! Look at your partner and yourself as God's "works of art" that exceed the world's priceless paintings and irreplaceable sculptures.

Remember, you are not the highest level on the evolutionary scale. You "...are his workmanship, created in Christ Jesus unto good works, which God hath before ordained that we should walk in them" (Eph. 2:10).

Personal Reflections

Now that the premarital session or the Bible Study is over, reflect on what you have learned.

Children and Parenting

Study Seven

The purpose of study seven is to explore what God teaches about children and parenting. There are seven biblical principles that are essential to raising children, and numerous passages that answer the question, "How can I make him mind?"

Raising children is not easy. In *Masterpiece* magazine, John F. MacArthur, Jr. says,

> Parents today face a much more difficult task than their parents: how to raise godly children in an increasingly evil world. While the world may have changed, God's Word hasn't. It clearly shows us how to provide shade for our children. An old Chinese proverb says "One generation plants the trees, and another gets the shade" …what kind of trees are we planting?[20]

Although the challenge of raising our children to the glory of God is a huge responsibility, thankfully God has not left us without an instruction manual. The Bible offers practical and effective principles and specific commands that can produce greater fruitfulness in our families.

CHILDREN

Look up the following passages and respond to each question regarding the preciousness, sinfulness, and humility of children.

PRECIOUSNESS OF CHILDREN

The Bible teaches that children are precious gifts from God, and parents are temporary guardians or managers of these little ones. It's important to remember that, ultimately, all children belong to God, and they are only on loan to the parents for a short time.

1. How are children described in Psalm 127:3, and what does it mean?

2. According to 1 Samuel 1:24–28, to whom do children belong? What are the implications for when they grow older?

3. Jesus healed children many times. Write out what the following passages teach:
    Matthew 17:14–18

    John 4:46–54

SINFULNESS OF CHILDREN

While it is true that children are precious gifts from God, they are born as sinners because the sin nature is inherited from our first parents, Adam and Eve. This is the reason why salvation is necessary. Every baby is born a sinner and needs God's full forgiveness.

1. What does Psalm 51:5 teach about newborn children?

2. How does Romans 3:23 describe all human beings?

3. Study 1 Samuel 2:12–4:18 and answer the following questions.

    A. What was wrong with Eli's sons?
        Example: They were wicked men who were religious, but they didn't know the Lord (2:12).

        2:17

        2:22

        2:25

    B. What sins did Eli commit?
        Example: He honored his sons more than he honored God (2:29).

        3:13

        3:18

        4:18

C. What should Eli have done differently? (These answers should
be the opposite of your answer to the question what sins did Eli
commit?)

D. If you were Eli, what would you have done differently?

HUMILITY OF CHILDREN

Childhood is not a disease! It is a special time when God works
with parents to bring children to spiritual, emotional, mental and physical maturity. Explore these passages and answer the following:

1. What does Jesus do with the children in Matthew 19:13–15, and
what is the importance of it?

2. What does Jesus say about the children, and what is the main idea
He is conveying?

Matthew 18:1–4

Luke 18:15–17

PARENTING

Parenting is a wonderful privilege and an awesome responsibility. It is not easy, but it can be extremely rewarding. In this section we'll examine infertility, God's directions for planning children, and the seven responsibilities of parenthood.

INFERTILITY

Infertility is the inability of a woman to conceive or of a man to impregnate. Some infertile couples sincerely want children. What should they do? Modern science offers alternatives to vaginal conception, but are they all morally right? Discover God's perspective on infertility.

1. Genesis 21:1–2; Hebrews 11:11

2. Genesis 25:21

3. 1 Samuel 1:11, 19–20

4. Luke 1:7, 13

If you are or become infertile, what will you do?

PLANNING FOR CHILDREN

Children should be wanted. For this reason, conception control could be used to space the years between the births of children and to enable you to plan when the children will be born.

I believe you should consult a medical doctor and request information on conception control. The methods should be openly discussed so that you and your partner both understand them completely. It is also recommended that you consult Ed Wheat's detailed information in chapter eleven of *Intended for Pleasure*. As a Physician, Wheat conscientiously explains the advantages and disadvantages of many conception control methods and devices.

There is a moral difference between birth control and conception control. Birth control allows conception to occur. One form of birth control is abortion, where the child is deliberately killed before it is born. Abortion is only one of the modern birth control methods. There are many other birth control methods and devices on the market today. These devices allow the sperm to fertilize the egg and for life to begin. Then, they discard or poison the fertilized egg in order to prevent the growth and birth of the child. These devices, like abortion, are the deliberate taking of a precious, human life. This is murder!

Conception control differs from birth control because it prevents the fertilization of the egg. This is accomplished by the blocking of the sperm from reaching the egg. Since life begins when the sperm fertilizes the egg, I believe that conception control is acceptable. You will need to pray, study the Scriptures, and decide for yourselves.

SEVEN PARENTAL RESPONSIBILITIES

This section focuses on seven biblical principles that can help you to become the parent that God has called you to be. These commands are not a menu to choose from. Instead, they point to seven areas that every parent must address.

1. In Deuteronomy 6:7, it says you are to **TEACH** your children. There are two extremes that need to be guarded against. One extreme is to teach little or nothing. Parents in this category feel it's the state's job to educate their children, and apart from potty training and very basic teaching, they leave the responsibility with

the state. Another unwise position is to teach children on the level you wish they were instead of where they really are. This extreme is illustrated by the following account.

> Matthew, my 3 1/2 year-old son, was eating an apple in the back seat of the car, when he asked, "Daddy, why is my apple turning brown?" "Because," I explained, "After you ate the skin off, the meat of the apple came into contact with the air which caused it to oxidize thus changing its molecular structure and turning it into a different color." There was a long silence. Then Matthew asked softly, "Daddy, are you talking to me?"[21]

While this is humorous, it's also sad because some parents actually talk to their children as inappropriately as this father did. Parents need to teach their children on appropriate levels that reflect the child's age and learning abilities. The level of teaching may be increased incrementally as the child matures. Parents will need to be sensitive to their children's learning styles and vary their teaching methodologies accordingly.

A. What will you teach your children besides how to eat, potty, talk, respect others, work hard, and use money wisely? Consider 2 Timothy 3:15, and list two specifics.

B. How will you teach these things to them? Remember that the church is a resource, and don't forget those unplanned moments that occur when major changes happen within the family.

2. In Proverbs 22:6, it says you are to **TRAIN** your children.

    A. How will your example effect them? List two ways.

    B. What's the relationship between your example and your instruction?

3. In 2 Corinthians 12:14, it teaches you are to **PROVIDE** for your children.

    A. How can you provide for their spiritual needs? List two examples.

    B. In what ways can you provide for their physical needs?

    C. What will you do to meet their emotional needs?

4. In Ephesians 6:4, it says you are to **NURTURE** your children.

    A. Nurturing your children means that you will raise them as disciplined and behaving children. How do you do it?

    B. In an article entitled "No God? No Problem: American Atheists Fight for the Right not to Believe," the New Jersey State Director for American Atheists speaks about his marriage and family. Staff writer Michael Riley states "David says his daughter will be raised to respect both her mother's Jewish beliefs and her father's atheist outlook. When she is old enough, she'll decide which path to follow."[22]
    Identify and explain three areas that will be problematic for the parents and for the child due to this position.

Problem areas for the parents:

Problem areas for the children:

5. In 1 Timothy 3:4, it says you are to **CONTROL** your children.

    A. How will you control your children? List two examples.

    B. In what ways can you accomplish this in each area?

6. In Titus 2:4, it teaches you are to **LOVE** your children.

    Although this is addressed to mothers, fathers are to love their children too. What can you both do to ensure that you will love your children as God intends? Provide two examples.

7. Proverbs 3:11-12 teaches that God chastens and corrects His children as a father chastens and corrects his son. Therefore, it is necessary for you to **DISCIPLINE** your children by chastening and correcting them. Discipline, which involves the setting and enforcing of standards, is essential for civility.

    World magazine reports that

    > Montana, the only state with no specified daytime speed limit, must change its laws after the Supreme Court ruled its "reasonable and proper" rule was too vague; motorists, the court ruled, had no objective standards for compliance with the law.[23]

    This illustrates the universal need for objective standards and appropriate punishment when they are neglected. In Proverbs, parents are given specific instructions on administering loving discipline. Write out what each verse teaches parents to do.

13:24

19:18

22:15

23:13

29:15

29:17

A. Discuss child discipline with your partner. Write out several responses to the question, "how does God want us to discipline our child(ren)? Engaged couples should answer in the future tense, "After marriage, we will…"

B. If you choose to follow God's directions in using appropriate physical discipline, the positive results will become evident. Your children will know their boundaries, your expectations, and the consequences that will be applied for disobedience. It is important to consider the child's age, sex, and offense when administering discipline. For example, teenagers should not be humiliated by treating them like little babies. Parents need to ask what is valuable to each child and design the discipline appropriately. It is important to remember that no two children are the same and what works with one child may not be as effective with another child. While God's objective standards never change, the methods behind their implementation may vary from child to child.

When my children were young, they each had a chart hanging in their room with chores listed, the times and dates that the chores had to be completed, and the consequences if the chores were not completed on time. There was no guessing on what Dad and Mom wanted from them. Both of our boys knew what was expected, when it was expected, and what would happen if they were disobedient.

Contemplate each statement and provide a thoughtful response.

1. *Age appropriateness* – Teenagers are too old to be spanked, and creative punishments need to be applied by the parents.

2. *Gender appropriateness* – Fathers should avoid spanking their daughters when they begin to physically mature.

3. *Offense appropriateness* – Parents do not need to spank their children for every act of disobedience. Parents need to vary their methods of discipline and use physical discipline as one method among a variety of others.

SUMMARY

Raising children is both a wonderful privilege and an awesome responsibility. It involves communicating values and demonstrating them before your child's ever observant eyes.

The Word of God clearly teaches that children are gifts from God and they belong to Him. These little ones are lent to parents for a short time, but they ultimately belong to God. You are responsible to bring them to spiritual and emotional maturity.

Parenting is not easy, but it is richly rewarding. Nothing in life can bring more satisfaction than for a parent to see his child living close to the Lord and serving Him.

The responsibilities of parenthood are numerous, but seven have been addressed in this study. These include the responsibility to teach, train, provide for, nurture, control, discipline, and love your children. The Scriptures abundantly instruct you to physically discipline your children. Additionally, it is essential for you to balance your methods of discipline and employ creative ways to motivate your children to willingly obey.

Last, but not least, your example must imitate Jesus Christ. Your life teaches more clearly than any amount of words ever could. The Bible says, "Be ye, therefore, followers of God, as dear children; and walk in love…" (Eph. 5:1–2a). As you follow God, your children will follow you; but if you ignore God, then they will probably ignore Him too!

Personal Reflections

Now that the premarital session or the Bible Study is over, reflect on what you have learned.

Marital Roles, Relationships, and Responsibilities

Study Eight

In study eight, we will concentrate on the roles of the husband and the wife, the type and quality of a God-honoring relationship, and the specific responsibilities that are outlined in the Bible. The conflicting positions of egalitarianism and complementarianism will be explained.

Have you ever noticed that some couples get along extremely well while other couples seemingly never get along?

> My husband's two friends delivered a briefing while taking a course on tactical operations. When they were through, the instructor said the presentation was good, but it had failed to distinguish between engagements and battles. The teacher grew frustrated when no one in the class volunteered to explain that a battle is a series of smaller engagements. "Everyone was responsible for last night's assignment" he said. "Surely someone knows the difference." "I know," my husband finally offered. "An engagement is what precedes the wedding, and the battle is what follows."[24]

It does not have to be like this and hopefully your experience is, or will be, different. Of all the topics in this manual, none is more questioned and controversial than this one. Why? America is changing. Comparing our society fifty years ago to the society of today yields lightning bolt results. In the 50's, America was predominantly made up of white, middle-class, and one-income households in which people identified with the characters in televisions shows like "Father Knows Best" and Ward and June Cleaver on "Leave it to Beaver." Dad was the breadwinner and Mom was the bread baker. Couples averaged two children, one car, and one dog. Life seemed slower, streets were safer, and almost everyone experienced some sense of community life.

Today it's different. America is multi-cultural, multi-lingual, and multi-income. Fewer parents are living with their adult children, and nursing homes have picked up a mammoth business. The havoc of divorce has left broken families in its wake.

Some families are working three or four jobs, two for Dad and one for Mom, with one of them dabbling in something on the side. Other families have a stay-at-home Dad who cares for the home and children while Mom competes in the corporate jungle. Humanists suggest that since society is different, the standards should be different. This is relativism. According to the Bible, God's standard never changes; what changes is the application and implementation of the unchangeable standards. One example of societal change is "At-Home Dads Gather and Bond," where "the third annual At-Home Dads Convention in Des Plaines, Illinois, affirmed the [existence of] 1.9 million fathers who are caregivers to their children."[25]

Nevertheless, even though society is continuously changing, God's biblical standards for male and female roles, relationships, and responsibilities remain intact as the objective yardstick for families. This is true whether "family" means a single Dad and his son, a single mom and her daughter, or a husband and wife with children.

YOUR ROLES

The roles of males and females are being debated. There are two primary views. D. A. Carson defines them as the following:

> "Egalitarians" believe that the Bible teaches that men and women are so equal that no distinctions in role should be maintained – whether in home or in church or elsewhere – that are grounded in their respective genders. "Complementarians" hold that the Bible teaches equality of importance and significance (for both are made in the image of God), but that distinctions are made that assign complementary roles in home and church.[26]

The "complementary" view is in harmony with the grand concert of Scripture. There is no room for contention or competition between the sexes. God created women and men as absolute equals and neither is inferior to the other. The two sexes were designed so each partner would fulfill God's purposes and provide companionship for the other. God's plan is for husbands and wives to become one, like interlocking pieces of a jigsaw puzzle. They are to mirror the relationship that Christ, the Bridegroom, has with His Church, the Bride. The emerging picture portrays inseparable oneness and absolute unity.

The Bible reveals God's specific instructions for both sexes. What does God say in the Bible about how husbands and wives are to relate to one another? This section will explore three primary passages from the Bible that will clarify God's directions for the husband and wife relationship.

1 Peter 3:1–7

1. What does God teach about the equality of the sexes?

2. What does this look like in life, and how should it affect your present, or future marital relationship?

3. What is the wife's role as seen in verse 1?
    See also Ephesians 5:22–24; Colossians 3:18

4. Describe the beauty outlined in verses 3–4, and explain why this is valuable? See also Proverbs 31:10–31. A wise sage said, "No cosmetic for the face can compare with the beauty of inner grace" (anonymous).

5. From verse 7, what will happen to the prayer life of a husband who treats his wife in an ungodly way? Compare Psalm 66:18.

1 Timothy 5:1–2

1. How are younger and older women to be treated?

2. How are younger and older men to be treated?

Ephesians 5:2–6:4

1. What does 5:21 say about mutual submission, and how can you apply it? Compare 1 Peter 5:5.

2. According to 5:22–24 and 33, what is the role of the wife?

3. What is the role of the husband as outlined in 5:23–24? Consult 1 Corinthians 11:7–8.

4. According to 5:31 (see also Genesis 2:24), how do you, or will you, relate to your in-laws? This is crucially important, so answer it fully after you have discussed this with your partner.

   a. *For Him*: Regarding her family, indicate what your relationship is, or will be. Include dependence, support, fellowship, and the amount of contact.

b. *For Her*: Regarding his family, state the quality and quantity of time you are, or anticipate spending with his family.

c. *For Both*: How do or will you handle holiday visits and special family get-togethers? Look at your calendars and chart where and when you could go for one year. List the holidays and where you might be.

YOUR RELATIONSHIPS

1. Love is giving, not getting (John 3:16). Love is the highest priority, and it will continue throughout eternity (1 Corinthians 13:8). How much, or in what way, is a husband to love his wife?

   A. In Ephesians 5:25?

   B. In Ephesians 5:28?

C. In Ephesians 5:33?

2. How are wives to relate to their husbands according to Titus 2:4?

3. How would you describe the relationship of husbands and wives according to Genesis 2:18, 24?

4. Specify how you agree or disagree with the following statement. God calls husbands to gently lead their life partners in a humble and God-fearing way. They are to model the servant-leadership of Jesus. Wives are called by God to eagerly walk in submission with their husbands so non-believers will immediately recognize that they are modeling the relationship of Jesus' bride, the Church, to Jesus Christ. Married couples must be *dependent* on the Lord, *interdependent* upon one another and independent from their parents.

5. From Deuteronomy 24:5, a bridegroom was excused from the military and all business for one year so he could spend his first year of married life uninterrupted with his new wife. What does this imply about newly married couples?

6. In Malachi 2:14–16 God judged Israel for the mistreatment of their wives. What did they do, and how does this relate to you? See 3:5.

YOUR RESPONSIBILITIES

This is a difficult area because no matter what position one takes, there are always couples who do not fall within these parameters. One example is a marital situation in which the wife works and the husband keeps the house because of a physical disability that prevents him from working outside of the home. Another illustration is of a single mother, or a divorcee who must work in order to support herself and her family. Barring these and other exceptions, the author believes the primary responsibilities of husbands and wives are as follows.

1. What is the husband and father's responsibility according to 1 Timothy 5:8?

2. What should the husband and father provide in each category? These categories are the four areas that Jesus grew in. "And Jesus increased in wisdom (intellectual) and stature (physical), and in favor with God (spiritual) and man" (social) (Luke 2:52).

    Spiritually –

    Socially –

    Intellectually –

    Physically –

3. What are the wife's primary responsibilities according to Titus 2:4–5?

4. 1 Timothy 5:14 addresses widows; but applying it to all married women, what responsibilities do you see?

5. Does this make the mother the children's primary care giver? Why or why not? See also Ephesians 6:1–4.

6. If the wife works outside of the home, what additional responsibilities could the husband assume so both partners have equal free time? Discuss this with your partner, and write out what you both are willing to do.

SUMMARY

The world is changing, but truth never changes. What was true yesterday is true today and will be true tomorrow. God's Word is true, and it is unchangeable.

The Bible provides the boundaries for the roles of husbands and wives. Each partner in the marital relationship is equal but different. Within these differences, God has determined the roles for each. Husbands and wives are to submit themselves to God and to one another. Their union is an equal partnership where each has specific assignments. Husbands and wives must learn to depend upon one another and not to burden their aging parents with responsibilities that they must assume themselves.

The type of love that God has for each is the type that husbands and wives must learn to develop and practice daily. The wife must submit to her husband with the same willing spirit that she submits to the Lord. She is to manage the home and make whatever changes are necessary in order to provide an adequate and comfortable living environment. The husband is to lead his wife in genuine humility, remembering that he will give an account to God for how he has treated his wife, and that his prayers will go unanswered if he fails to relate to her as God requires. Furthermore, the husband is required to provide for his wife and children.

Husbands and wives have a wonderful opportunity to raise children so that they will believe in God and follow Him. This mutual responsibility is a high priority in Scripture and must be constantly worked on so the children are taught and trained according to the Bible. Solomon reminds all parents, "A wise son maketh a glad father, but a foolish son is the heaviness of his mother" (Proverbs 10:1).

If Christian husbands will lovingly and humbly lead their wives, and if Christian wives will lovingly and willingly submit to their husbands, then divorce will be less common among believers. Both husbands and wives need to remember, "I can do all things through Christ, who strengtheneth me" (Philippians 4:13).

Prayer is central in developing and maintaining God-honoring relationships. Pray for and with your partner so you can understand where and how God desires you to change!

Personal Reflections

Now that the premarital session or the Bible Study is over, reflect on what you have learned.

Our Money

Study Nine

What does God say about money and financial responsibility? Study nine will guide you through numerous passages that reveal God's teaching on money, work, taxes, giving, debt, and budgeting. Included in this study is a sample form that you may use to create your own budget. Add or delete areas that are not applicable to you and your partner. Remember that in marriage there is no "mine" or "yours." There is no place for individual accounts. Couples must blend their assets so that everything becomes "ours."

Some people are cracker-jacks with money and others can't remember to record the checks they write in their check register. Which one is most like you? There was a husband who prided himself in his financial savvy. His wife purchased an expensive personal item and afterwards felt guilty that she had splurged. Cooing in her husband's ear, she bargained, "Let's just consider this my next Valentine's Day present." "No way!" her husband retorted. "That was too expensive – I'll have to buy you something else." Obviously he did not realize what he had said.

The Bible teaches the real value of money and many practical principles on financial responsibility. God's Word addresses your need to work, pay taxes, and support His church. Furthermore, the Scriptures outline God's teaching on personal debts. The following passages will provide you with a wealth of wisdom to apply in your marriage.

BIBLICAL PRINCIPLES ON MONEY
How valuable is money?

A wise person said, "Money will buy a bed but not sleep; books but not brains; food but not appetite; finery but not beauty; a house but not a home; medicine but not health; luxuries but not culture; amusements but not happiness; religion but not salvation; a passport to everywhere but heaven" (anonymous). Money is a means to an end, but never an end in itself.

THE OLD TESTAMENT

The Old Testament reveals six general principles about money. List those principles after you've read each passage.

1. Deuteronomy 8:17–18; 1 Chronicles 29:12
   Example: God is sovereign over money

2. 2 Kings 5:20–27

3. Psalms 49:17; Proverbs 27:24

4. Psalms 49:6–11

5. Ecclesiastes 5:19

6. Ezekiel 7:19

THE NEW TESTAMENT

The New Testament contains valuable teaching on money. Study the following passages and write out everything they teach about money.

1. Luke 12:13–21

2. 1 Timothy 6:7–8; see also Philippians 4:11–12

3. 1 Timothy 6:10

4. 1 Timothy 6:17–19

In addition to these general principles, the Bible addresses work, taxation, giving, and debt. Read the passages in each category and answer the following questions.

WORK

What does God say about work?

1. Proverbs 6:6–8.

2. List four principles from 2 Thessalonians 3:7–12.

TAXES

What do the Scriptures teach about taxes?

1. Matthew 17:24–27

2. Matthew 22:15–22

3. List four principles from Romans 13:1–7.

GIVING

What are God's directions for giving?

1. Malachi 3:10

2. Mark 12:41–44

3. 1 Corinthians 16:2

4. 2 Corinthians 9:6–7

DEBT

Read the verses, and write out why you agree or disagree with the statements.

1. Avoid continuous debt. See Proverbs 22:7 and Romans 13:8.

2. Live contentedly within your means. Compare Luke 3:14 and Hebrews 13:5.

3. Plan major purchases in advance and count the costs carefully. See
    Luke 14:28-30.

4. Resist impulsive buying. (To control her addiction to shopping,
    one woman kept her credit cards frozen in a large bowl of water.
    By the time she thawed out the ice, the urge to splurge passed, and
    she was in better control of herself.)

    You would be wise to identify couples that are faithful stewards
and are financially successful. Ask these godly people for practical
advice and list their suggestions.

    You have learned many helpful principles from the Holy Bible
about money. Now it's time to apply them by establishing a workable
budget.

PRACTICAL STEPS TO BUDGETING

It is valuable to remember, "If you aim at nothing, you would be sure to hit it" (anonymous). A budget is an aim, or a goal. It collates what comes in and goes out, and it displays what is left over. Occasionally someone will say he does not need a budget. This may be because he does not know how to make a budget, or he refuses to monitor his own finances. In marriage, there is no room for independent or unwilling attitudes. Both partners need to mutually agree on how much will be spent, by whom, when, and where.

When my wife and I married in 1977, we established a budget and agreed upon a set amount each could spend without conferring with the other. This simple agreement saved us countless problems.

You and your partner need to see two pictures clearly in order to accurately project a workable budget. First, you must add up your combined assets and income to form your total assets. Second, you need to arrive at your combined indebtedness and expenses to form your total liability. Subtracting the liabilities from the assets reveals a true picture of your financial status. Carefully research your finances and fill in the amounts. If you are a single income family, combine the liabilities and use your single income figure in the budget.

OUR COMBINED ASSETS

Total Value

1. Home(s) (If you hold a mortgage, subtract the mortgage from the current actual value.)
   _____
2. Vehicle(s) (include vans, motorcycles, boats and trailers)
   _____
3. Account(s) (include Savings, Stocks, Bonds, and Funds)
   _____
4. Life Insurance and retirement (include Standard and Roth IRA's and 401K's current redemption value)
   _____
5. Loans due you
   _____
6. Valuables (include furs, jewelry, stamps, coins, or sports memorabilia)
   _____
7. Other (include anything of value not covered above)
   _____
8. Total (Put this figure on the worksheet.)
   _____

OUR JOINT INCOME

Total Value

1. Husband (net amount)
   _____
2. Wife (net amount)
   _____
3. Both: (include alimony, child support, businesses like Avon, Mary Kay, Tupperware, Real Estate or disability payments)
   _____
4. Other: (include any income not outlined above)
   _____
5. Total (Put this figure on the worksheet.)
   _____

Now that you have determined your assets, consider your liabilities.

OUR TOTAL LIABILITY: DEBTS AND EXPENSES

This is designed to be a beginning budget. Numerous items may need to be added or deleted as you age, birth or adopt children, continue on with your education, and eventually retire.

	Monthly	**Annually**
1. Your local church (10% of gross)		
2. Rent or house payment		
3. Utilities (heat, electricity, water, and garbage removal)		
4. Household (furnishings & repairs)		
5. Telephone (include cellular, pcs, pager and internet service)		
6. Vehicle(s) (include payments, insurance, repairs, and gas)		
7. Food, vitamins and health needs		
8. Clothing		
9. Insurances (include fire, health, dental, and life)		
10. Loans(s) (student and personal)		
11. Credit Cards		
12. Alimony or child support		
13. Recreation and vacation		
14. Savings (10% of net)		
15. Allowances for both		
16. Subscriptions (magazines, journals, and newspaper)		
17. Membership dues		
18. Clubs (book, music, and video)		
19. Cable (television and internet)		
20. Total (Insert this figure on the worksheet.)		

Although this is tedious, it is necessary. Someone said two could live as cheaply as one. The only two who can do that is a dog and his flea. For everyone else, the costs mount up.

Comparing your assets against your indebtedness clarifies what you have to work with and provides a realistic picture of your finances. Fill in the worksheet below.

PERSONAL WORKSHEET

Assets			
Income	+ _____		
	_____	= Total Assets	$ _____
Indebtedness			
Expenses	+ _____		
	_____	= Total Liability	$ _____
Total Assets	_____		
Total Liability	- _____		
Working Capital	_____		

Now that you have a budget, you must work at making it work. This means that you will need to discipline yourself to spend only the amounts that you and your partner agreed for each area. This may not be easy, but it is possible.

One way you can keep your debts under control is to only charge items that you can pay off during the credit card "grace period." This amount of time varies with each card. If you do this, then you can avoid paying the high rate of credit card interest.

It is essential for you to learn to live within your income. This will be challenging, but you can do it. It's important for you to eliminate impulse buying. Plan what you want to spend, save up for it, and then make the purchase. With a few exceptions like houses and cars, you can do this by God's power.

SUMMARY

Money can lead to spiritual struggles. Three times God's Word records that Jesus said, "It is easier for a camel to go through the eye of a needle, than for a rich man to enter into the kingdom of God" (Matthew 19:24; Mark 10:25; Luke 18:25). This repeated emphasis shows that money is a problem for most people. The apostle Paul reminds us that, "For the *love of money* [emphasis mine] is a root of all evil: which while some coveted after, they have erred from the faith, and pierced themselves through with many sorrows" (1 Timothy 6:10). Spiritual struggles result from the misuse and abuse of money.

Study nine has led you through the passages that teach the value and proper use of money. You have learned God's views on work, taxes, debt, budgeting, and giving. Now it is up to you. You and your partner must learn how to live within your means. One way to do this is to agree not to buy on impulse. Your purchases should be planned, and some items should be saved for and purchased later. This requires discipline; but with God's help, you can handle your finances in a God-honoring fashion.

Lastly, separate bank accounts must be closed. There is no room for individual accounts in Christian marriage. You and your partner have, or will, promise yourselves to one another for the rest of your lives. Do you remember your vows? Part of it is, "...to have and to hold, from this day forward, for better for worse, *for richer for poorer* [emphasis mine], in sickness and in health, to love and to cherish, until we are parted by death; as God is my witness, I give you my promise."[27] Be careful not to allow money to become a wedge between you and your partner. Become one – in your finances too!

Remember to pray together over your finances. God is interested in everything that you do. Avoid the error of praying over spiritual matters and handling your finances in the flesh. Pray over your bills and ask God for practical wisdom so you can make the right choices. God can and will help you!

Personal Reflections

Now that the premarital session or the Bible Study is over, reflect on what you have learned.

Conflict Resolution

Study Ten

A wise person said, "there is a big difference between the wedding veil and the garbage pail" (anonymous). After the honeymoon comes the day to day reality of life. This is when the marital bliss fogs, in the mist and haze of realized mutual imperfections.

Couples have inevitable conflicts. But what does a couple do when they disagree and are in face to face conflict? Your answer may determine whether you will enjoy a beautiful marriage or a struggling relationship. You need to expect conflicts and prepare yourself to disarm them so they will not be destructive. This requires spiritual and emotional maturity.

MATURITY IN MARRIAGE

Luke said, "And Jesus increased in wisdom and stature, and in favor with God and man" (2:52). These four areas Jesus grew in were intellectual (wisdom), physical (stature), spiritual (favor with God), and social (and man). Couples need to grow in all four areas. You may be mature, but do you have enough maturity to develop a spiritually healthy marriage?

WHAT IS MATURITY?

- Maturity is the ability to control anger and settle differences without violence.
- Maturity is patience. It is the patience to pass up immediate pleasure in favor of a long term gain.
- Maturity is perseverance, the ability to sweat out a project or a situation in spite of heavy opposition and discouraging setbacks.
- Maturity is the ability to face unpleasantness and frustration, discomfort and defeat, without complaint or collapse.
- Maturity is being big enough to say, "I was wrong." And when right, the mature person need not experience the satisfaction of saying "I told you so."

- Maturity is the ability to make a decision and stand by it. The immature spend their lives exploring endless possibilities, and then doing nothing.
- Maturity means dependability, keeping one's word, and coming through in a crisis. The immature are masters of the alibi. They are the confused and the conflicted. Their lives are a maze of broken promises, former friends, unfinished business, and good intentions that somehow never materialize.
- Maturity is the art of living in peace with what we cannot change, the courage to change what should be changed, and the wisdom to know the difference (anonymous).

WHO ARE THE IMMATURE?

The immature are possessive. Their sense of security is frequently in question, and they think they must control their partner. This possessiveness can smother the other person and tempt him to respond in anger or frustration. The immature are manipulative. In order to control their spouse, they feel they must arrange circumstances like they arrange furniture. The immature are habitually in conflict and repeatedly in trouble. Controlling spouses eventually crush the precious life out of a relationship. The original love may ooze out like peanut butter escapes a squeezed sandwich. Immature couples obviously have a greater difficulty in marriage.

Do you see yourself? Do any of the above descriptions depict you or your partner? If so, wait! Wait until you are both ready. Marriage is not easy, and healthy relationships do not simply happen. Marriage is hard work. But it is worth it. If you and your partner are both mature, then proceed forward. If you're not spiritually or emotionally equipped, wait a while. Remember that the mature person can wait.

A ONE-EYED MARRIAGE

In 1976, my wife-to-be and I participated in premarital counseling with the late Dr. Watson Pindell at Washington Bible College. Wise as a modern day Elijah, Dr. Pindell told me, "Craig, while you're dating keep both eyes open. After you get married, shut one eye." At the time, it made little sense; but after the wedding, I got the idea. One annoying habit my new wife had was to shut the bureau drawers all but an inch. Every time I went into the bedroom, I immediately saw these half-opened drawers. Don't laugh. I'm perfectly serious. For a while it was a monumental problem, but I eventually remembered Dr. Pindell's advice and I shut one eye. Guess what happened? I could not see the drawers any longer. That happened in 1977, and I am still shutting half-opened drawers. The difference is it does not bother me any more. In all fairness, my wife has had to shut one eye too. I'm sure there have been numerous times when she has had to shut both eyes.

UNDERSTANDING BIBLICAL PRINCIPLES NECESSARY FOR CONFLICT RESOLUTION

This is where the rubber meets the road. Your level of maturity will surface during this process, and the real you will soon be evident. Conflict resolution requires four steps that must be done in a certain order and done completely. There are no short cuts to resolving difficulties biblically. These four steps include communication, confession, the granting and receiving of forgiveness, and spiritual renewal.

STEP ONE OF FOUR: COMMUNICATION

In order to resolve your conflicts, you must communicate with one another. Resolution is impossible unless both of you are willing to open up and talk honestly. But resolution is possible when both partners are willing to work towards resolving their differences. This is more than simply vocalizing words. Study the passages and identify the principles of communication.

1. Psalm 19:13–14

2. Ecclesiastes 5:1–7

3. Matthew 12:34–37

4. Ephesians 4
    A. v. 15

    B. v. 25. Example: There is no room for deception, exaggeration, embellishment, or intentional manipulation in a spouse's communication. Speaking the truth means speaking truthfully, without adding or leaving out any important facts.

    C. vv. 26–27

    D. v. 29

    E. vv. 31–32

5. Philippians 4:8. (Remember, we speak from our *thoughts!*) This area cannot be overestimated. Someone correctly said,

> Just one little sin, what harm can it do? But give it free reign and soon there will be two. And then sinful deeds and habits ensue, *so guard well your thoughts*, or they'll destroy you (*Our Daily Bread*).

6. Colossians 3:8–10. In this passage, Paul uses the metaphor of putting off and putting on, like you would change a soiled garment.

Therefore, step one to resolving conflicts is to communicate in a God honoring way. But how can you do this when you are angry? More will be said about that later.

STEP TWO OF FOUR: CONFESSION

What is biblical confession? J. Gordon Henry clarifies, "Biblical confession is necessary for cleansing and renewal. Confess means to acknowledge sin by owning up to whatever the sin is in agreement with God and saying the same thing about the sin that God has said."[28] No redefining, denying, or hiding your transgressions. Confession is simply agreeing with God and stating the identical thing He says in the Bible about your wrongdoing.

Delineate what truths are portrayed in these Scriptures.

1. Ezra 10:11

2. Nehemiah 9:1–3

3. Proverbs 28:13

4. James 5:16

5. 1 John 1:9–2:2

Confession to God and to one another is central to resolving your marital conflicts. Before you can be forgiven by God or your spouse, you must be willing to admit your wrongdoings and call your behavior what it is – sin!

STEP THREE OF FOUR: FORGIVENESS

Conflict resolution necessitates a granting of and receiving of forgiveness. What does God say about forgiveness?

1. Psalm 32:1–2

2. Psalm 130:3–4

3. Isaiah 38:17

4. Isaiah 44:22

5. Jeremiah 31:34

6. Matthew 18:21–35

7. Mark 11:25–26 (Repeated in Matthew 6:14–15 and Luke 6:37.)

8. Luke 17:3–4

9. Ephesians 4:32

These passages reveal that God forgives people who have changed their minds and their behaviors. Furthermore, you have learned that you must forgive your spouse in the same way that God has forgiven you. Only after you have been forgiven and you have granted forgiveness, are you ready to proceed to the next step in conflict resolution.

STEP FOUR OF FOUR: RENEWAL

Renewal means that you're getting your relationship back on track and that you are relating to each other as God directs in His Word. This fourth step is crucial. Notice what God says concerning renewal.

Write out what God says in the following passages.

1. Matthew 5:23–24. Example: Renewing a relationship is a higher priority than worship. These verses teach that you must be reconciled first, then you can come and worship. In marriage this means that couples must settle their differences before coming to Church. It's pointless to worship if you're nursing a grudge or harboring resentment against your spouse in your heart. Settle it, and then come and worship God!

2. Matthew 18:15–17. This passage points to church discipline, but it is applicable to marriage because it identifies who should go to whom when one is offended, and what the goal must be.

3. 2 Thessalonians 3:14–15

4. Galatians 6:1–2

5. 1 Corinthians 11:31

6.   1 Peter 4:17

7.   Matthew 7:3–5; Luke 6:41–42

APPLYING PRINCIPLES TO ACHIEVE RESOLUTION

You have learned many biblical principles regarding communication, confession, forgiveness, and renewal. Now it's the right time to
put these truths to work in your relationship.

COMMUNICATION: THE CONFERENCE TABLE

Couples must communicate, and one effective way is to set up a
Conference Table.[29] A conference table is a pre-determined place
where you and your partner go to address a problem without attacking
one another. The rules for the conference table include: 1) no loud
voices, 2) no name calling, 3) no attacking one another, 4) no regurgi-
tation of former offenses that have already been resolved, 5) begin
with your own weaknesses and sins first (see passage number 5 under
Renewal, above), 6) start and end with genuine prayer, 7) read Ephesians 4:17–32 before every Conference Table, 8) focus on the problem
and how you may mutually solve it, 9) be willing to compromise and
avoid the, "it's my way or the highway" attitude, and lastly, 10) demonstrate agape love for one another by giving more to your partner
than you take from him or her!

The process to follow is to confess your areas of weakness and to
humbly ask God for His forgiveness. Afterwards, you need to admit
your weaknesses to one another and to ask your partner to forgive you.
Mature Christians do not deny, cover up, or withdraw within themselves. They do not excuse or defend their actions. Furthermore, they
do not erect a minefield of defenses. Humble partners seek to reconcile
by realizing their sins and repenting. Repentance is a change of mind
that leads to a change in behavior. It involves sensing remorse or sor-
row for your sin. Genuine repentance will result in your willingness to

change. Some changes may happen immediately while other changes will occur incrementally. Simply saying "I'm sorry" or "I apologize" is not adequate because these common phrases are not biblical words for repentance, and they do not include a promise to remember the sin no more. True relationships are built upon honesty before God and honesty with another. If you are honest about your sins, you will sincerely seek true and lasting reconciliation with God and with your partner.

Newly wedded couples would be wise to have a conference table every day for the first year of marriage. It is a practical way to nip conflicts in the bud. After you have been married many years, you will habitually do this and your level of communication will increase. Whether marital veterans or newly wedded, all couples should schedule a conference table when it is needed!

FORGIVENESS: ITS APPLICATION IN MARRIAGE

God requires you to forgive others as He has forgiven you (Ephesians 4:32). Surveying God's forgiveness yields three principles. First, God will never use your forgiven sins against you in the future. Second, God will not communicate your sins to anyone else. Third, God will not dwell on your sins Himself.

In *Redbook* magazine, Susan Gifford offers "22 Ways to Pamper Your Marriage." Her suggestions show the opposite of biblical Christianity. She states one way to pamper your marriage is to gossip. "Talk about his brother's numbingly, dull girlfriend, your best friend's marriage troubles, his best friend's wife. Men like burrowing around in the dirt at least as much as we do...you're just amusing yourselves, not rumor mongering."[30] Gossip is never right and must be avoided. If you really have forgiven your partner, as God has forgiven you, you will never repeat a matter or betray your partner's confidence.

Some say God forgives and forgets. God definitely forgives, but does He forget? God has chosen to purposefully dismiss your sins from His conscious thoughts so He does not harbor your sins in His mind to use them against you. This means He does not dwell upon them like children dwell upon what they suppose they will get for Christmas. They are still there, but God refuses to think about them. In this way, you are commanded to forgive as God forgives. You are instructed to grant forgiveness freely, and to discipline yourself to guard your mind against focusing on another's sins that you have forgiven. Furthermore, you may not resurrect them for future condemning or judging of your spouse. You must discard them from your mind like you take out the trash.

RENEWAL

You have already studied several verses on renewal and seen its importance. To get a solid handle on it, study the book of Philemon. It's short, but it contains volumes of practical insights on genuine restoration and renewal. Onesimus was Philemon's runaway slave who got saved under Paul's ministry (v. 10). Paul counsels Onesimus to voluntarily return to Philemon (v. 12), and Onesimus obeys, returning with Tychicus and a letter (the book of Philemon). In this letter, Paul makes several requests of Philemon.

1. Paul appeals to Philemon on what basis, or in what? v. 9

2. What does Paul ask Philemon to do concerning Onesimus? v. 12

3. How is Philemon to receive Onesimus? vv. 16–17

4. What have you learned about forgiving, forgetting, and renewing?

5. In Ephesians 2:3, you were once labeled a "child of wrath," but in John 15:14 you are called a "friend." In 1 Peter 3:7 you are called "heirs," and in Luke 8:21, Jesus describes you, saying, "My mother and brethren are these who hear the word of God and do it." How does this relate to the story of Philemon?

6. How will you apply this in marriage?

SUMMARY

Blessed are the couples that can resolve their conflicts. Effective conflict resolution is one of the keys to spiritually healthy and happy marriages. Spiritual maturity is necessary because immature persons often attack each other, instead of addressing their conflicts. Study ten has focused on four steps to resolve marital conflicts.

The first step is communication. Partners must learn to communicate and to use words and expressions that build up one another and do not tear down, cut up, or accuse one another. Couples also must learn to resolve their conflicts daily and not to allow anger to build up day after day. To accomplish this, the author has prescribed a conference table that you should participate in often. It is important that you adhere to the ten rules for the conference table that were explained in the study.

The second step of conflict resolution is confession. This is more than saying, "I'm sorry," or "I apologize." Confession means to agree with God and to say the same thing that he says about your actions. If He calls it iniquity, you must agree with Him and confess it to Him as iniquity. There is no room for denying or redefining sin.

The third step to conflict resolution is the granting of and receiving of forgiveness. Christians are commanded to forgive as they have been forgiven. Their forgiveness is not an option. God said that He forgives you if you will forgive one another. Conversely, God will not forgive you if you refuse to grant forgiveness. Furthermore, you may not limit your forgiveness or make it conditional. Forgiveness must be free and without any strings attached.

When you forgive someone, essentially you are promising three things. First, you will not use that person's sin against her in the future. Once it is forgiven, it is never to be spoken of again. Second, you will never tell anyone about the sin. This eliminates the temptation to gossip. After a sin is forgiven, it can never be shared with anyone. Third, you are promising that you will not dwell upon that sin. This is difficult but it can be done through the power of the Holy Spirit. God lives in every believer, and He enables Christians to live the Christian life. With God's strengthening power, you can put forgiven sins behind you. Someone said, "[What is the] formula for a happy marriage? It's the same as the one for living in California: when you find a fault, don't dwell on it" (anonymous).

The fourth step is spiritual restoration and renewal. There was one situation in which a husband committed adultery and the wife forgave him. Their marriage continued many years afterwards. From the outside everything looked normal. But the opposite was true. The wife said, "I cannot forget, it can never be the same between us." In her mind, she had forgiven her husband; but in reality, she had not. Obviously, there was no restoration or renewal in their relationship. If she had biblically forgiven him, and their relationship was spiritually restored, then it would have looked quite different.

This means she would have refused to dwell on the memory of her husband's past unfaithfulness, and she would have received him in love. One writer said, "Some say forgive and forget. Love remembers and forgives anyway" (anonymous).

It is hard to put some things out of your mind because Satan constantly brings them up over and over again. But God commands you to both forgive and love your partner. This involves not allowing those nagging recollections to occupy your mind. These demonic reminiscences must be driven out of your mind. Once these monstrous memories are expelled, then you will be able to lovingly restore your erring partner and renew your commitment to one another. This spiritual renewal will enable you to build your relationship upon biblical forgiveness and spiritual restoration. The result will be a spiritually galvanized marital union!

Pray with your partner, and together ask God to enable you to resolve your differences. Do not forget that the Christian life cannot be lived by the flesh, but only by the power of God in you.

Personal Reflections

Now that the premarital session or the Bible Study is over, reflect on what you have learned.

APPENDIX ONE

The Equality of Women

In our *Age of Information*, the Church faces new and fresh challenges in communicating truth. But is it ready? A major problem facing the Church is the redefining of manhood and womanhood until they are now almost indistinguishable. This unisexual blending has gravitated from the barbershop to the House of Worship. Even those who are not redefining the roles of the sexes are confused and unprepared to articulate what they believe are the God-given roles, relationships, and responsibilities of each gender. This appendix is designed to communicate and clarify the spiritual, social, and Christian service opportunities for women from a biblical perspective.

Women are equal to men. God said, "... as being heirs together of the grace of life..." (1 Peter 3:7). Some have misunderstood the Bible and thought that God had assigned a lower status to women than to men. This is false. While some world religions may teach this, the Bible does not! God created women and He designated them as equal heirs to all spiritual blessings and benefits for all eternity!

Women are to be respected by men. God requires believers to relate to one another as family members. God commands, "Rebuke not an elder, but entreat him as a father; and the younger men as brethren; the elder women as mothers; the younger as sisters, with all purity" (1 Timothy 5:1–2). This means that women, irrespective of age, are to be highly regarded. There is no room for male's superior attitudes, inferior appraisals, sexual exploitations, lustful longings, belittling comments, or degrading remarks. All of this is sinful and must be avoided. Occasionally, married women are treated differently than single women. This does not please God. All women whether married, single, divorced, separated, or widowed must be shown God-honoring respect! With God, there are no exceptions. Christians must learn not to make any exceptions either!

Is there a difference between what men and women should do in the local church? Some say yes, while others say no. Professing believers hold to opposing views. D. A. Carson offers,

117

"Egalitarians" believe that the Bible teaches that men and women are so equal that no distinctions in role should be maintained – whether in home or in church or elsewhere – that are grounded in their respective genders. "Complementarians" hold that the Bible teaches equality of importance and significance (for both are made in the image of God), but that distinctions are made that assign complementary roles in home and church.[31]

Which view is biblically accurate? The biblically correct view is the "Complementary View," based upon Genesis 2:18–25, 3:16; 1 Timothy 2:9–15; 1 Corinthians 11:3, 7–9; Ephesians 5:22–33 and Colossians 3:18–19. This means that females are absolutely equal to males, but their roles in life are distinct and different from the males. Consequently, their roles in church are equally distinct and different too. As a result, women should not serve in areas of the church in which they exert authority over men. Some feel this may limit women's Christian service. But the Bible is abounding with ministries women can do very well.

These worthwhile ministries include, but are not limited to, showing hospitality to strangers, nursing the sick and raising children (1 Timothy 5:10), showing kindness to the poor (Proverbs 31:20), and opening their homes to the needs of the church (Romans 16:3–5). Teaching, counseling, mentoring (other women, teenagers, and children, Titus 2:3–5), singing, testifying, and praying are more key areas where women may excel. Women can effectively minister to people's needs by visiting in hospitals, unwed mothers' homes, mental institutions, orphanages (James 1:27), nursing homes, women's prisons (Matthew 25:34–40), and juvenile detention centers.

Godly women have been in the past, continue to be in the present, and will be greatly used in the future by God to accomplish His will on earth. It is clear that being a woman is not an inferior position, but it is a God appointed honor!

Women, enjoy being what God made you and who you are, and rejoice in how He can use you for His glory in and outside of His church.

APPENDIX TWO

What About Divorce and Remarriage?

In contemporary society, divorces are increasing at an alarming rate. Couples who struggle within their marriages are not limited to the unsaved, the poor, or the uneducated. The deterioration of marriages is occurring globally, and in every economic, cultural, and social tier. Divorce has escalated to pandemic proportions. Like the place and purpose of spiritual gifts, divorce and remarriage divides Christians. Some ask, "Are you better off with him or without him?" For them, the biblical teaching on divorce and remarriage is a moot point! Others inquire, "Do you meet the biblical conditions for divorce?" citing the exception clause recorded in Matthew 19:9. Still others exhort that all divorce is sinful, regardless of the circumstances. What is right?

A brief review of three biblical principles will be enlightening. *First*, God hates divorce. The Bible teaches, "For the LORD, the God of Israel, saith that he hateth putting away" (Malachi 2:16). God has chosen the heterosexual marriage as the clearest earthly reflection of the divine picture of Christ as the husband and the church as His bride. God hates divorce because it tarnishes the perfect picture of the eternal relationship that we have with Him and He has with us. Can you imagine Christ divorcing Himself from His own bride, the Church? Certainly not! *Second*, God the Son was questioned about divorce. He was asked, "Is it lawful for a man to put away his wife for every cause?" (Matthew 19:3). Jesus responds by quoting, and thus authenticating, Genesis 1:27 and 2:24. These verses explain two truths, 1) God created male and female human beings, and 2) God's purpose was for them to be one in a life long marriage. *Third*, Jesus summarizes this dialogue with his critics by saying, "What, therefore, God hath joined together, let not man put asunder" (Matthew 19:6). This should have settled the question, but it didn't. The quibblers continue, asking, "Why did Moses then command to give a writing of divorcement, and to put her

119

away?" (v. 7). These faultfinders are citing Deuteronomy 24:1–4, to which Jesus answers, "…because of the hardness of your hearts" (Matthew 19:8).

It is obvious that divorce was permitted, but was never God's directive will! What does this mean? Simply that God permitted it, but did not ordain it. God will grant rebellious and persistent humans their desires (Psalm 37:4), even if it is their bad decisions. The Israelites demanded a King (1 Samuel 8:5), but God warned them that this was not a wise choice (vv. 11–17). He told them why it was a bad choice and what a human King would do to them. Nevertheless, they persisted in their open rebellion against the revealed will of God, and He gave them a King (vv. 19–22). This was not what was best for them, but it was the desire of their wayward and sinful hearts.

The exception clause is similar, and it is an example of God's permitted will. Divorce is not, nor has it ever been God's directive will! The exception clause was permitted due to the hardness and sinfulness of human being's rebellious hearts. What should we do? Should Christians divorce one another on the grounds of adultery? Some will say "yes" because of Matthew 19 and 1 Corinthians 7. Others will say "no" because they interpret these passages differently. I am encouraging you to consider reconciling with your spouse. You would be wise not to consider divorce as a viable option. Nadine Crenshaw, a romance writer, shows her children "How to Find True Love," and offers five practical suggestions. One of them is profound. Nadine says,

> Talk about everything – except divorce. I was not a talker when I met your dad. In my childhood, I'd learned that it was best to remain silent around my alcoholic father, who could twist any statement into a weapon. But Robert stubbornly refused to accept my silence. It was my first intimation of the strength of his love. There is only one subject, we discovered, that should be taboo in a marriage: divorce. The mere mention of this word brings it into the realm of possibility. Your father and I learned this the hard way. During a trying period years ago, I found myself calmly saying, "Maybe we should get a divorce." He answered,

"Maybe we should." How did we get to that point? Simply by mentioning the ugly "D" word in times of anger ("If we can't work things out we might have to consider divorce") and by slipping it sideways into discussions ("If we ever get a divorce…"). The day we finally confronted the divorce option, we were not terribly angry with each other, but we had gradually let divorce become a real choice in our thinking. We made a pact, then and there, never again to mention the word "divorce" in association with us. We haven't dared break that pact in 17 years.[32]

Nadine Crenshaw is wise because she realizes the value of silence on the divorce issue. Christians should be silent about this too! The "D" word should be stricken from your vocabulary, and the subject should be taboo in all Christian homes.

Dear friend, do not consider divorce! The devastation of divorce on you, your children, and the Church's witness to the world could be atrocious! Pray for the strength to work out your problems. Seek out caring, biblically based marriage counseling. Talk with someone whom you respect, and hold yourself accountable to him or her. While divorce on the biblical grounds of fornication (Matthew 19:9) is permitted, it is neither expedient (1 Corinthians 6:12; 10:23) nor recommended.

The word for "fornication" from the original language that the New Testament was written in is transliterated *porneia*. It is translated "fornication" in the New Testament. Greek scholars define it as, "…prostitution, unchastity,… [and] of every kind of unlawful sexual intercourse."[33] Further, porneia may be understood as, "…unfaithfulness of a married [man or] woman."[34]

Fornication is an evil work of the flesh and must be avoided (Galatians 5:19; Acts 15:20, 29). The Christian's physical body is "for the Lord" and it is not to be engaged in fornication (1 Corinthians 6:13; Ephesians 5:3). Fornication invokes God's wrath because it is contrary to His will; and fornicators must repent of this evil practice (Colossians 3:5–6; 1 Thessalonians 4:3; Revelation 9:20–21). Failing to repent of fornication will result in the judgment of God (Galatians 5:19–21).

Friend, if you are tempted to engage in fornication, ask for help from a godly Christian. If you are already in a sinful relationship, repent today. Refuse to see him or her. Confess your sin, forsake it, and be reconciled to God. If you are married, go back to your partner. Be honest and seek reconciliation with him or her. God is pleased with obedience, but He is greatly displeased with disobedience.

What is God's will if you married, and then one of you became a believer? Is it God's will for you to rid yourself of this pagan, non-believer? Some think so and justify their divorce on the grounds that God does not want them to be unhappy. They insist that God wants them to be happy and free. Carefully consider God's Word before you form your opinion. God says,

> And unto the married I command, yet not I, but the Lord, Let not the wife depart from her husband: But to the rest speak I, not the Lord: If any brother hath a wife that believeth not, and she be pleased to dwell with him, let him not put her away. And the woman which hath an husband that believeth not, and if he be pleased to dwell with her, let her not leave him. For the unbelieving husband is sanctified by the wife, and the non-believing wife is sanctified by the husband: else were your children unclean; but now are they holy. But as God hath distributed to every man, as the Lord hath called every one, so let him walk. And so ordain I in all churches. Is any man called being circumcised? let him not become uncircumcised. Is any called in uncircumcision? let him not be circumcised. Circumcision is nothing, and uncircumcision is nothing, but the keeping of the commandments of God. Let every man abide in the same calling wherein he was called. Art thou called being a servant? care not for it: but if thou mayest be made free, use it rather. For he that is called in the Lord, being a servant, is the Lord's freeman: likewise also he that is called, being free, is Christ's servant. Ye are bought with a price; be not ye the servants of men. Brethren, let every man, wherein he is called, therein abide with God (1 Corinthians 7:10, 12–14, 17–24).

One of my precious friends is unequally yoked to a non-believer. As a godly woman, she prays for her husband and witnesses to him by her holy, wholesome, and God-honoring lifestyle. What does someone who is in the muddy trenches of an unequally yoked marriage think about remaining continuously married to a non-Christian? She writes,

> For the woman who was already married, and then became born again afterwards, please consider this. Do not look for a new husband because you think the Lord must want you to leave, since you are now unequally yoked. You can be blessed within your own marriage as you apply godly principles and hold tight to the One who has saved you. The Lord knew before you did what would happen. Therefore, trust in Him to make you into what He wants you to be – exactly where you are!

This dear saint is brightly shining in the enveloping darkness. Like a pristine spring flower, she is blooming in the desert exactly where God planted her. If she can blossom, then you can too!

What about remarriage? If you are a Christian widow, widower, or one who divorced according to biblical grounds, then biblically you may remarry another believer. But be cautious. Previous mistakes may continue in endless repetition, like the cycle of sin-repentance-and-deliverance in the book of Judges, unless you have learned from your mistakes and made the necessary adjustments.

One common fallacy is that some remarrying couples mistakenly think that they do not need counseling before the wedding, since they were married for many years. Couples remarrying need premarital counseling as much as first time engaged couples, in order to identify past sins and replace them with godly actions. If they do, then they can break out of their habitual cycle and experience an excellent marriage!

Marriage as Worship and Witness

Have you ever considered marriage as worship? Contemporary churches are redefining worship, and the bookstores are filled with books describing what constitutes worship. But what does God say about worship, and how does it relate to marriage? Furthermore, how can a marriage lead others to Christ?

Let's answer these questions by considering three issues. *First*, we will examine 'What is Worship.' *Second*, we will see how worship relates to marriage. *Third*, we will focus on how biblical marriages are a model for struggling Christians and a powerful witness to non-Christians.

WHAT IS WORSHIP?

God's love is limitless and His affections are boundless. Throughout the unfolding history of redemption, He has tenderly cared for those who trust and honor Him. As the Supreme Being, He expects your acknowledgment of His worth in your life. This spiritual worship is described in the following ten explanations.

Worshipping God is expected. The Psalmist declares, "…he is thy Lord; and worship thou him" (Ps. 45:11). God is worthy of your worship, and God expects you to worship Him. In the book of Revelation, the angel directed John not to worship him, but to worship God (19:10). God is calling you to worship Him! Heed His call. Worship God!

Worshipping God means honoring Him. The author of 1 Chronicles reminds us, "Give unto the LORD the glory due his name…worship the LORD in the beauty of holiness" (16:29). Christians owe God adoration and praise simply because He is God. Worship God by honoring Him!

Worshipping God means to fear Him. David explains, "But as for me, I will come into thy house in the multitude of thy mercy: and in thy fear will I worship…" (Psalm 5:7). It is important that you understand the difference between yourself and God. The two of you are worlds apart. God is intrinsically holy, and you are holy only because God declared you so when you put your faith in His Son. Worship God by fearing Him!

Worshipping God involves listening to Him and obeying Him. Moses' successor, Joshua, was a godly military leader who loved God wholeheartedly. When the "captain of the host of the LORD" confronted Joshua, he fell on his face and worshipped. God told him that the city of Jericho would be given to him. Joshua listened intently and rigorously obeyed. As a result, God's will was fulfilled and "…the LORD was with Joshua, and his fame was proclaimed throughout all the country" (Joshua 5:13–6:27). The lesson is that authentic worship involves listening to God and following His directions. God is still speaking through His written Word today. Worship God by listening to and obeying Him!

Worshipping God means loving Him. When Jesus was praying, He said, "And this is life eternal, that they might know thee the only true God, and Jesus Christ, whom thou hast sent" (John 17:3). In order to love God, you must first know Him. He has revealed Himself in His written Word so you may see Him as He is. After you become rightly related to Him through His Son, Jesus Christ, then your love for God can grow in intensity and allegiance. As it does, your testimony may be that of the Psalmist, who said, "I love the LORD, because he hath heard my voice and my supplications" (Psalm 116:1). As a reminder, God commands His people to love Him (Deuteronomy 6:5), and Jesus identifies this commandment as the first and greatest commandment (Matthew 22:37). Worship God by loving Him!

Worshipping God involves humbling yourself before Him. The writer of Psalm 95 invites you, saying, "O come, let us worship and bow down: let us kneel before the LORD our maker" (v. 6). Humans do not control the universe or the affairs of earth. God is the Creator, and He made all that exists out of nothing. Consequently, genuine worship means you will humble yourself under His awesome power. Worship God by humbling yourself before Him!

Worshipping God must be voluntary. When the wise men came from the East to worship Jesus in Jerusalem, they said, "...[we] are come to worship him" (Matthew 2:2). These men came willingly and traveled a significant distance just to worship Jesus. This means that your worship of Jesus Christ should be voluntary and arise from your own holy motivation. Some people worship only by coercion or manipulation. For example, some husbands attend church reluctantly with their wives, or some wives begrudgingly accompany their husbands. But under these circumstances, worship is insincere, and this does not please God. He wants you to want Him! God longs for indisputable worship that springs from spiritual hunger and thirst. Worship God by voluntarily seeking Him.

Worshipping God means worshipping God alone. Throughout biblical history, God's people frequently fell into worshipping idols. Jesus said, "Thou shalt worship the Lord thy God, and him only shalt thou serve" (Matthew 4:10). Is it any different today? Protestant churches can fall into the worship of idols too. The next time you are in church, ask yourself, *who or what am I worshipping?* Some worship the people, others worship programs, while still others worship the music. Guard your heart and take spiritual inventory. Make certain that you worship God and only God! Worship God by declaring your faith, hope, and love to Him alone!

Worshipping God must be done in spirit and in truth. Jesus said, "...true worshippers shall worship the Father in spirit and in truth: for the Father seeketh such to worship him. God is a Spirit: and they that worship him must worship him in spirit and in truth" (John 4:23–24). Furthermore, Paul clarifies, "For we are the circumcision, which worship God in the spirit, and rejoice in Christ Jesus [who *is* the truth, John 14:6], and have no confidence in the flesh" (Philippians 3:3). This means that true worshippers must worship God as He has revealed Himself in the Holy Scriptures. David declares, "I will worship...and praise thy name for thy loving-kindness and for thy truth..." (Psalm 138:2). Worship God in spirit and in truth by worshipping Him as the one and only true God!

Worshipping God must emanate from a heart full of faith. This means that spiritual worship must be the outflow of a life that is bubbling over in belief. Paul stood before Governor Felix in Caesarea and answered charges that Tertullus made against him. Paul responded, "But this I confess unto thee, that after the way which they call heresy, so worship I the God of my fathers, believing all things which are written in the law and in the prophets: And have hope toward God…that there shall be a resurrection of the dead, both of the just and unjust" (Acts 24:14–15). Paul had hope because Paul believed in the triune Godhead: Father, Son and Holy Spirit! God wants you to worship from a heart of faith, hope and belief. Worship is the ripe and natural fruit that grows on the life of faith! Worship God by believing Him by faith!

These ten principles are humbly offered and are not intended to be exhaustive. But they are important truths that you need to apply daily. As you absorb them and integrate them into your life, your spiritual worship will be purified, and God will be glorified.

THE RELATIONSHIP OF
WORSHIP TO MARRIAGE

Dave and Debbie were marriage partners who filed for divorce out of frustration and despair. As the inevitable severance drew closer, they became involved with a Christian couple. In time, they envied the other couple because the other couple had what Dave and Debbie longed for, but could not find. One day, this distraught couple asked the other couple, "How can you be so happy and contented?" Slowly, and patiently, the other couple witnessed about Jesus Christ, and Dave and Debbie were wonderfully saved.

Although it did not occur overnight, in time Dave and Debbie changed the ways that they were habitually responding to each other. Then their lives were different, and their relationship improved dramatically. One Friday, the lawyer called and said the divorce papers were ready for their signatures. Thankfully, the couple changed their minds about getting a divorce, and Dave ran the divorce papers through his shredder. Today, Dave and Debbie are growing closer to God and to each other. God has rewarded them with two beautiful little girls. Their lives have never been the same since Jesus Christ became their Savior.

This account is fictitious, but it represents hundreds of lives and dozens of marriages that I have seen changed. Marriage is not as much about finding the right person as it is about being the right person. Both Dave and Debbie had ugly areas in their lives, and each needed the transformation that only God can bring. After they both trusted in Christ, God changed them internally. With God's help, they were able to achieve a rewarding marriage, because God was at the center of it. No longer was each person vying for the control of the marriage. Eventually, Dave and Debbie began to worship God in the ways described in this book. The closer they came to God, the closer they came to each other. They worshipped not only in church, but also in their home because they were listening to and obeying God as a family.

What is the relationship of worship to marriage? If both partners worship God, as He desires, then your marriage can be the way God intended! This is true because the closer you come to God, the closer you will be to each other.

MARRIAGE AS A WITNESS

Mature and godly Christian couples are desperately needed in today's churches. This is because many young couples marry, and they are unprepared for the inevitable conflicts that will arise. These younger couples need older couples for encouragement and godly advice. I am convinced that the most effective way to help younger married couples is by linking them to mature, mentoring couples that can gently guide, practically instruct, and meaningfully pray with them.

Mentoring is a biblical model of personal one-on-one instruction. Paul told Titus that, "The aged women [were to] teach the young women to be sober, to love their husbands, to love their children, To be discreet, chaste, keepers at home, good, obedient to their own husbands, that the word of God be not blasphemed" (Titus 2:3–5). The early church enlisted women to help women. This same type of spiritual oversight is direly needed in the modern church, where mature couples can take young couples under their wings and help them mature in Christ by spiritually mentoring them.

The unsaved world needs Christian role models who live what they believe. Like the previously mentioned Dave and Debbie, unsaved couples can benefit from seeing marriages lived as God designed. This is true because examples are more caught than taught. It is like the missionary who was told by a native, "Don't tell me how to live. Show me how to live."

In conclusion, excellent marriages are for the sake of you, the church, the world, and God.

Excellent marriages are for your sake because if you maintain one, then you can fulfill your God-ordained role in the world. Paul said, "I therefore, the prisoner of the Lord, beseech you that ye walk worthy of the vocation which ye are called" (Ephesians 4:1). Your vocation or role is to be the spiritual salt and light in a dark and deteriorating society. What will occur when Christians fulfill their roles? They will be filled with the joy and satisfaction that comes to those who know and do God's will. May we be like John who said, "…that our joy may be full" (2 John 12).

Excellent marriages are for the sake of the church because the church is only as strong as the members that comprise it. With rock solid marriages, the church will be sturdy and able to withstand the demonic attacks of the evil one. Furthermore, younger couples will have mentoring couples to identify with, learn from, and to imitate.

Excellent marriages are for the sake of the world because they demonstrate the hope that the world so desperately needs. When failing couples observe successful couples, it stimulates them to have the hope that with Christ, they too can overcome their dilemmas.

Last, but not least, **excellent marriages are for God's sake** because He designed them and expects humans to achieve them. God is glorified when a couple puts Him first and relates as He directs!

My prayer is that you will mature in your spiritual lives and in your marriages so you can declare what Jesus proclaimed when He asserted, "The Father hath not left me alone; for I do always those things that please him" (John 8:29).

Recommended Books and Tapes

There are a number of practical books to help you become what God has intended for you to be. For every chapter, I will list a few suggestions. For complete publishing information see the Bibliography on page 151.

The Foundations for Marriage

To better understand the biblical foundation for the prohibition against being unequally yoked, study Exodus 34:16; Joshua 23:12–13; Ezra 9:1–15; and Nehemiah 13:23–27. For a detailed explanation on divorce and remarriage, see Appendix 2, page 120.

George, Elizabeth. *A Woman After God's Own Heart* and *Beautiful in God's Eyes*.

> In *A Woman After God's Own Heart,* Elizabeth George focuses upon "The Pursuit of God," "The Pursuit of God's Priorities (Her Husband, Her Children, Her Home, Her Self, and Her Ministry)" and "The Practice of God's Priorities." What does it mean to have a heart after God's heart? What does it involve? The author answers, "As you desire all that God desires, love all that He loves, and humble yourself under His mighty hand (1 Peter 5:6), then your heart will indeed be a heart after God. What a blessed thought!" (p. 54). Excellent! In *Beautiful in God's Eyes,* she expresses the awesome truth and beautiful description of a godly woman from Proverbs 31:10–31. Ladies, this is an exceptional book!

Heald, Cynthia. *Loving Your Husband.*

> Each of the 12 lessons follows the format of "Insight into Scripture, Insight in Myself, Insight into My Husband," and "Insight from an Older Woman." In lesson 3 entitled "I Will Make Him a Helper," Heald quotes

Ruth Bell Graham, who clarifies, "We women learn from the Bible that God created us to be a 'help meet' for our husbands (Genesis 2:18). That is, a help suited to their needs. Since every man is different, needs will vary. So it is up to the wife to study her own husband to discover how she can best meet those needs" p. 35.

Jenkins, Jerry B., ed. *Families: Practical Advice from More Than 50 Experts.*

An encyclopedia of family advice, *Families* contributors include Barna, Trent, McDowell, Ziglar, Wright, Gaither, Hansel, and many others. This tool is a hardback exceeding 300 pages.

Lewis, C. S. *Mere Christianity.*

This is a timeless classic that every Christian needs to read. Lewis explains Christianity in a style all his own. Writing on Christian Marriage, Lewis pens, "The inventor of the human machine was telling us that its two halves, the male and the female, were made to be combined together in pairs, not simply on the sexual level, but totally combined" (p. 88). Highly recommended!

Lovett, C. S. *Unequally Yoked Wives.*

Dated, but the thesis is biblical and the content is practical. Lovett suggests "The Nutcracker Technique," (p. 38) where one arm of the nutcracker is "light" and the other is "works." His idea is that Christian wives should gently squeeze their non-Christian husbands (represented as the nuts) between the handles of "light" and "works" until their hard shell cracks. This will expose the "meat" of the nut, which represents the soul of the unsaved husband. The analogy is that once the shell is open, the exposed soul will respond to the convicting work of the Holy Spirit.

MacArthur, John, Jr. *Answering the Key Questions About the FAMILY.*

This is a good book to hand out. It's only eighteen pages, but offers helpful insights.

—*Different By Design: Discovering God's Will for Today's Man and Woman.*

Arranged in three parts, "The Attack on God's Design, God's Design for Marriage, and God's Design for the Church," MacArthur looks at the big picture of how and where males and females fit into God's grand design.

Roberts, Lee. *Praying God's Will for My Wife.*

In "For Men Only," Roberts reminds Christian husbands that, "The single most important thing that you can do for your wife is to pray for her. Praying for your wife is more than a privilege. It is a responsibility and one that you...must not take lightly. Begin today...and you will soon see dynamic growth take place in her life, in your marriage, and in her as the wife that God desires her to be" p. v.

Wheat, Ed and Gloria Okes Perkins. *The First Years of Forever.*

Detailed and complete, this tool is highly informative. Includes recommended cassettes and videocassettes.

Love

Keller, W. Phillip, *A Layman Looks at the Love of God: A New Devotional Study of 1 Corinthians 13.*

Practical and understandable, Keller links the understanding of Christ's character to grasping the real meaning of love.

Missler, Nancy. *Why Should I Be The First To Change?*

This brief paperback is a powerful tool, showing how God healed a marriage and taught the husband and wife to truly love one another. Missler reassures, "I am now not only getting God's love, as I remain an open and cleansed channel for Him to use, but I am also getting all the human, emotional love from Chuck that I ever desired in the first place" (p. 109).

Sweeting, George. *Love is the Greatest.*

This book is highly practical and oriented toward application. Sweeting reminds us, "Even the nicest, friendliest person becomes hard to love sooner or later. Just about the time you think you really love someone, you discover in an outbreak of hostility that you still have a long way to go...you learn that natural love does wear thin. Human love simply is not enough to cope with the pressures of daily living" (p. 20). Sweeting does not leave you hanging, but provides steps to help you apply the written Word so you'll be able to love others with God's pure, action-oriented love.

Zodhiates, Spiros. *To Love Is To Live.*

A hardback over 350 pages, this is a helpful commentary on 1 Corinthians 13. Commenting on "Love...thinketh no evil," (13:5d), Zodhiates says, "Let us be careful not to use memory as a ledger of the evil we observe and the injuries we receive. If your actions and thoughts today are colored by resentment and spite because of what someone has done to you, you cheat yourself of one possible pleasant thought, one bit of heaven. To the bitter heart, the sunshine is no longer bright, the song of the bird is not musical, and a pocketful of gold brings no ... contentment" (pp. 137–138).

Pamela, my wife and best friend, recommends the following:

Bloem, Diane. *A Woman's Workshop on Proverbs.*

—with Robert C. Bloem. *A Woman's Workshop on Bible Marriages.*

Boone, Shirley. *One Woman's Liberation.*

George, Elizabeth. *Women Who Loved God.*

Kuyper, Abraham. *Women of the New Testament.*

Price, Eugenia. *God Speaks to Women Today.*

Smith, Joyce Marie. *Esther: A Woman of Courage.*

Smith, Kenneth G. and Floy M. *Learning To Be A Woman.*

Tada, Joni Eareckson. *Secret Strength.*

Perception and Sensitivity

Adams, Jay E. *The Biblical View of Self-Esteem, Self-Love, Self-Image.*

> This valuable classic teaches how and why the love of self is idolatrous. Adam's teaching on the concept of the self-image is the clearest biblical explanation on the subject. Highly recommended.

— *Marriage, Divorce, and Remarriage.*

> Adams says, "Since this description of marriage focuses on covenantal companionship, it is obvious that one must cultivate companionship. A marriage lacking companionship is headed toward misery and divorce. All that jeopardizes companionship must be avoided; whatever promotes it must be cultivated" (p. 20). Very helpful.

Lloyd-Jones, D. Martyn. *Spiritual Depression: Its Causes and Cures.*

> This is a series of 21, non-outlined sermons delivered at Westminster Chapel. Lloyd-Jones is a deep writer who may be understood by those who are avid readers. Writing on 2 Timothy 1:7, Lloyd-Jones says it is both a reprimand and a reminder to Timothy. He clarifies "...if we suffer from this particular manifestation of spiritual depression, [it] is our failure to realize what God has given us, and is giving us, in giving us the gift of the Holy Ghost. You are gripped by the thing [fear]; you do not stop to remind yourself of who you are and what you are, this thing overwhelms you and down you go" (pp. 99–100). Illuminating!

Pratt, Richard L., Jr. *Designed for Dignity.*

> This book unearths the golden nugget of truth that our self-image must be the product of our personal relationship with God. We were designed for dignity because God designed us in His image and His likeness. For a full review, see my book review in *Food for the Flock,* July 1993, p. 20. Insightful.

Thurman, Chris. *Self-Help or Self-Destruction?*

> Thurman address ten psychological myths that he says, "...could destroy your life." These myths include "People are basically good; You need more self-esteem and self-worth; You can't love others until you love yourself; You shouldn't judge anyone; All guilt is bad; You need to think positively; Staying in love is the key to a great relationship; You have unlimited power and potential; and lastly, God can be anything you want Him to be." Highly recommended.

Communication

Adams, Jay E. *Shepherding God's Flock.*

> At first glance you might surmise that this is a book for preachers only. I suggest that it should be used in a wider context and that couples can benefit from it too. Chapter 8, "Communication in the Body," teaches a communication principle that couples need to master in order to grow in their lifelong relationship. Highly recommended.

Mack, Wayne A. *A Homework Manual for Biblical Living.* 2 vols.

> Volume 1 focuses upon personal and interpersonal problems, while volume 2 aims at family and marital problems. Arranged as workbooks to be completed and discussed, these are tools to do life-changing Bible study. Nearly every verse in the Bible on communication is covered in volume one, and needful suggestions

are gratuitously offered. Highly recommended with the hope that you will eventually complete every action-oriented chapter.

—*How to Develop Deep Unity in the Marriage Relationship.*

Unit 4 is entitled "Unity Through Communication" and takes you through several dozen passages so you will understand marital communication from God's perspective. Another part focuses on listening and offers detailed instructions on how to improve your ability to listen. Highly recommended.

Wright, H. Norman. *Communication: Key to Your Marriage.*

This is a must read for all married couples because it is brief, intensely practical, and humorous. Wright effectively communicates with cartoons. These cartoons allow couples to pinpoint their weaknesses so they may correct them. One cartoon has a couple sitting at a table saying simultaneously, "I know you believe you understand what you think I said, but I'm not sure you realize that what you heard is not what I meant." Another cartoon shows what ultimately could happen when a couple fails to communicate. A woman is sitting across from a Marriage Counselor and is saying, "When I got married, I was looking for an ideal – then it became an ordeal, and now I want a new deal." Humor aside, Wright offers helpful advice and provides worksheets for couples to complete and discuss together later. Highly recommended.

Consideration

White, Jerry. *Honesty, Morality, & Conscience.*

Honesty must be a central issue in your marriage. White says, "What you do speaks so loudly I can't hear what you say," and comments further "…actions make a deep impression…which no amount of words can alter" (p. 100). White is right! Actions do speak louder than words. Highly recommended.

—and Mary. *The Christian in Mid Life.*

Someone has coined the phrase; "The only constant is change." This is true in Christian marriages. Jerry and Mary outline mid-life changes in men, women, singles, and couples. They assert that married couples change and their expectations and expressions of need change too. The Whites explain twelve changes young couples usually make when they reach mid-life. The Whites offer practical ideas and helpful suggestions to equip you in overcoming these age-oriented changes and to meaningfully relate to one another. Good.

The Journal Of Biblical Counseling
JBC at Christian Counseling & Educational Foundation
1803 E. Willow Grove Ave., Glenside, PA 19038
215.884.7676; fax 215.884.9435
www.ccef.org or CCEFmail@aol.com

A Biblically based journal that does not substitute psychology for God's instructions on life. Some recent topics addressed include, "Understanding and Solving Anger Problems," "Counseling Singles," "Helping 'Psychologized' Counselees," and "Attention Deficit Disorder." Excellent material.

Marital Sexuality

Wheat, Ed and Gaye. *Intended For Pleasure.*

Textbook quality, but readable style. Ed is a medical doctor and gives sound advice. Chapter eleven explains conception control with the advantages and disadvantages of each device. Highly recommended for every Christian, regardless of how long you have been married.

Tapes

Wheat, Ed, M.D. *Love Life For Every Married Couple.*

Packaged in a two-cassette album, this is a must for newlyweds and any couple that desires to achieve sex as God intended. Topics include "How to build Physical Desire," "How to Bring Romance Alive," and "A Prescription for a Superb Marriage." Available from Scriptural Counsel, Inc., 130 Spring, Springdale, Arkansas 72764. 800.643.3477.

Wheat, Gaye. *Sex For Married Women.*

A godly woman tenderly speaks to the personal needs of Christian women. Excellent! Also available from Scriptural Counsel, Inc. 800.643.3477.

Additional Resources to Explore

Gallagher, Steve. *Tearing Down the High Places of Sexual Idolatry.*
Johnson, Rex. *At Home With Sex.*
Rosenberger, Margaret (compiler). *Issues In Focus.*

(Chapters 3, 4, and 12 are especially helpful.)

Smedes, Lewis B. *Sex For Christians.*
White, John. *Eros Defiled.*

Children and Parenting

MacArthur, John F., Jr. *Successful Christian Parenting.*

What do children need most? MacArthur says, "Self-esteemism is... unbiblical. Want to ensure that your child will become a delinquent? Feed his self-esteem and then compound the problem by refusing to correct him when he is wrong." He reminds parents that, "Your top-priority job as a parent... is to be an evangelist in your home...and point [your children] to Jesus Christ as the only One Who can save them." Highly recommended!

MacDonald, Gordon. *The Effective Father.*

The title could aptly be *The Effective Parent.* The book is built upon six principles which are, "If I am an effective father, it is –

"because I have deliberately set as one of my life's highest priorities the creation of conditions in my home that will stimulate my children to grow to their full human potential,

"because I have devoted myself to become an instrument and model of human experience to my children,

"because I have sharpened my sensitivity to my family's needs, committed my inner being to God's laws, and fixed a foresightful eye on opportunities and hazards ahead. I want to make sure that every family experience builds my children up and matures them,

"because I am filling my children's lives with perspectives and patterns which produce wisdom; I am lovingly purging their lives of unwholesome influences and tendencies that impede their progress toward maturity,

"because I accept and affirm my children for who they are, appreciate them for what they are accomplishing, and cover them with affection because they are mine,

"because I am aware that I always live on the edge of ineffectiveness and must continually reach out to God for wisdom and skill to accomplish my task." Superb!

MacMillan, Buechner, and Webb. *Action Guide for The Effective Father.*

This tool is a fill-in-the-blanks workbook that is forged around the six principles outlined within *The Effective Father.* Like condiments on a burger, this guide brings out the spiritual flavor and aroma of MacDonald's practical book. Highly valuable.

Additional Resources to Explore

Anderson and Miller. *Leading Teens To Freedom In Christ.*

Hromas, Roberta. *52 Simple Ways To Teach Your Child To Pray.*

Huggins and Landrum. *Guiding Your Teen To A Faith That Lasts.*

McManus, Richard C. *50 Practical Ways To Take Our Kids Back From The World.*

Peel, Bill and Kathy. *Where Is Moses When We Need Him: Teaching Your Kids The Ten Values That Matter Most.*

Powlison, David. *Pornography.*

Ray, Bruce A. *Withhold Not Correction.*

Tripp, Paul David. *Age Of Opportunity: A Biblical Guide To Parenting Teens.*

> A nine-part video series is designed to be used in conjunction with the book. It comes with a set of *Discussion Questions and Handouts* that can be used in a variety of settings. SDG Communications, 1998.

—*Teens and Sex*

Tripp, Tedd. *Shepherding A Child's Heart.*

> This is available as a book and also fifteen 30-minute video sessions with study guide.

Van Kooten, Tenis C. *Building The Family Altar.*

Wyrtzen, David. *Raising Worldly-Wise But Innocent Kids: Wisdom From The Book Of Proverbs For Modern Families.*

Helpful Magazines for the Family

Campus Life, a Christian magazine geared for Christian teenagers.

> CAMPUS LIFE
> P.O. Box 37057
> Boone, IA 50037-2057

Campus Journal, a quarterly devotional booklet that enables teenagers to practically apply the Word of God to their lives.

CAMPUS JOURNAL
Radio Bible Class Ministries
Grand Rapids, Michigan 49555

Christian Parenting Today, includes a column for single parents.

CHRISTIAN PARENTING TODAY
P. O. Box 37380
Boone, IA 50037- 2380

Useful Christian Websites for the Family

www.afo.net	American Family Online
www.cleanweb.net	A Christian web filter, advertising "We Take Out the Trash." There is a monthly fee.
www.crosswalk.com	Inspiration, information, and entertainment for the online Christian community.

Resources to Help You Use Your Computer for Christ

CHRISTIAN:

Baker, Jason E. *Parents' Computer Companion: A Guide to Software and Online Resources*

> Baker lists and explains hundreds of christian sites and resources that parents of all-aged children will appreciate. Practical Tool.

Hsu, Jeffrey. *Computer Bible Study.* Very practical.

Schultze, Quentin. *Internet For Christians*

> This is an excellent book that was written for two reasons. Schultze says, "First, to get you on the Internet. Second, to make you wise enough to be salt and light in

the new medium." See my review in "Worship Leader," July/Aug. 1996. Highly Recommended.

EDUCATIONAL:

The Internet For Dummies, Researching Online for Dummies, and *The Internet Kids & Family Yellow Pages.*

For simplification, IDG's "3-D Visual Series" books teach computer concepts with color pictures. Information is available at 800-434-3422. Helpful material.

Marital Roles, Relationships and Responsibilities

Elliot, Elizabeth. *Let Me Be A Woman.*

Peace, Martha. *The Excellent Wife.*

Piper, John and Wayne Grudem, ed. *Recovering Biblical Manhood & Womanhood: A Response to Evangelical Feminism.*

Nearly 600 pages, this expansive work is a classic on the sexes. Each essay stands alone so the reader does not have to read the entire book. Twenty-two evangelical, "Complementary View" scholars outline the biblical equality and role distinctions of both sexes. John Piper, commenting on masculinity, affirms "At the heart of mature masculinity is a sense of benevolent responsibility to lead, provide for and protect women in ways appropriate to a man's differing relationships." Regarding femininity, Piper continues, "At the heart of mature femininity is a freeing disposition to affirm, receive and nurture strength and leadership from worthy men in ways appropriate to a woman's differing relationships." Highly recommended.

Piper, John and Wayne Grudem. *50 Crucial Questions About Manhood and Womanhood.*

The Council on Biblical Manhood and Womanhood met in Danvers, Massachusetts in December of 1987. They produced *The Danvers Statement,* which says in part "Both Adam and Eve were created in God's image, equal before God as persons and distinct in their manhood and womanhood. Distinctions in masculine and feminine roles are ordained by God as part of the created order, and should find an echo in every human heart. Adam's headship in marriage was established by God before the Fall, and was not a result of sin" (p. 60). Excellent.

Priolo, Lou. *The Complete Husband.*

Ryrie, Charles Caldwell. *The Role of Women in the Church.*

An academic book that details the role of women from antiquity to modernity. Ryrie maps out the status of women in ancient Greece, Rome, Judaism, and private and public life. Scholarly.

Helpful Christian Magazines

Journal For Biblical Manhood and Womanhood, a brief but practical journal for men and women. They clarify, "The purpose of the Council on Biblical Manhood and Womanhood is to set forth the teachings of the Bible about the complementary differences between men and women, created equal in the image of God, because these teachings are essential for obedience to Scripture and for the health of the family and the Church" (Winter 1998, p. 2). Contact:

> The Journal for Biblical Manhood and Womanhood
> P.O. Box 7337
> Libertyville, IL 60048
> 888-560-8210

Today's Christian Woman, a high quality magazine for Christian women. Contact:

> Today's Christian Woman
> P. O. Box 37061
> Boone, IA 50037-2061

Marriage Partnership, a practical and insightful magazine for married couples. Contact:

> Marriage Partnership
> P. O. Box 37058
> Boone, IA 50037-2058

New Man: Proclaiming Life to Men, a Christian magazine geared particularly towards Christian men. Recent topics included "Born Again Sports. More superstars are mixing faith with their game." "Is this revival?" and "Win Your Childs Heart." Contact:

> New Man
> P. O. Box 420630
> Palm Beach, Fl 32142-8871
> 800-829-3371

Informative Web Sites

www.cbmw.org
> Council on Biblical Manhood and Womanhood. "Join us in our mission to teach what the Scripture teaches on manhood and womanhood."

www.bornagainmarriages.org
> "This ministry aims to strengthen existing marriages and to help couples on the brink of divorce."

www.maninthemirror.com
> A ministry to Christian men. (Pat Morley's ministry.)

www.desiringGod.org
> Helpful. John Piper's website. Complete with online books, articles, and useful information.

www.fellowshipassociates.com
> This ministry challenges the church and seeks to equip the church to become an irresistible influence. Robert Lewis's materials on Men's Fraternity is available here. Excellent.

Recommended Audio Tapes

Men's Fraternity by Robert M. Lewis. This 18-tape series is available through Fellowship Bible Church, 12601 Hinson Rd., Little Rock,

AR 72212. Westminster Seminary professor Peter Jones says, "His stuff is excellent. He gets 700 men at 6:00 AM every Wednesday morning to study manhood." He is on the board of CBMW (personal correspondence). Highly recommended.

Money

Burkett, Larry. *Your Finances in Changing Times.*

An entry-level book on Christian finances. One practical chapter asks, "What is financial Bondage?" (p. 62). The subtopics include physical, mental, and credit bondage; bondage through wealth, and the symptoms of bondage with sixteen conditions to evaluate if you are in financial bondage. Pertinently recommended!

—*Debt-Free Living.*

Dated, but extensive advice. Under "Where to Find Help," Burkett provides Appendix A to H with topics including "Credit Related Scriptures," "Your Rights Under the Fair Credit Reporting Act," "The Fair Debt Act," "The Consumer Credit Protection Act," "Introduction to Bankruptcy, Section 1," "Bankruptcy, Section 2," "Personal Financial Reorganization, Section 3," and "The taxpayers' Bill of Rights" (p. 6). Helpful.

Johnson, Albert J. *A Christian's Guide to Family Finances.*

This is a good tool with a leaders guide and transparency masters that are available from the publisher. Johnson's advice is helpful, but basic. Recommended for newlyweds and the financially inexperienced.

MacArthur, John F., Jr. "Whose Money Is It Anyway? A Biblical Guide to Using God's Wealth."

A practical book with a useful study guide included. The appendix is entitled "The Seductive Fantasy of Gambling." Excellent.

Conflict Resolution

Adams, Jay E. *The Jay E. Adams Pamphlet Series.*

There are six practical pamphlets in this series. Each one offers a Biblical explanation and application for each area that it addresses. These are valuable to carry in your Bible and to hand out to struggling couples. The titles include,

What Do You Do When Your Marriage Goes Sour?
What Do You Do When Anger Gets The Upper Hand?
What Do You Do When You Become Depressed?
What Do You Do When Fear Overcomes You?
What Do You Do When You Worry All The Time?
What Do You Do When You Know That You're Hooked?

—*The Christian Counselor's New Testament.*

Commenting on Luke 17:3–10, Adams teaches, "Forgiveness is not easy. Counselees must be taught to rebuke those who wronged them, and if they *say* that they repent, you must take them at their word and forgive them. This must be done no matter how often it occurs (vv. 3, 4). No excuses for failure to grant forgiveness will be accepted. It is not necessary to have more *faith* (vv. 5, 6) or to *feel like forgiving* (vv. 7, 9). Simple obedience is all that is needed (v. 10). Forgiveness is a promise to remember the sin against one no more. This promise is kept by (1) not reminding the offender of his sin, (2) not telling others about it, and (3) not dwelling on it yourself. If, when he is rebuked initially, he does not repent, the procedure in Matt. 18:15–17 must be followed. Cf. Mark 11:25" (p. 214). Solid teaching!

—*From Forgiven to Forgiving.*

Fitzpatrick, Elyse and Carol Cornish. *Women Helping Women.*

In a class all by itself, *Women Helping Women* seeks to motivate and educate women so they will meaningfully minister to one another. Sharon B. Covington reviewed

Women Helping Women in *The Journal of Biblical Counseling*. Sharon says, "But as I read and consider, I am stirred with longing to know the Bible better and to apply it with more wisdom as these women have done. I am challenged to prayerfully study and think through issues I have been content to avoid" (Vol. 16, No. 1, Fall 1997, 58–59). This is the type of response that Fitzpatrick and Cornish are seeking to stimulate. This book is a must-read for all Christian women who take Galatians 6:1–2 seriously and have the heart to reach out and help facilitate God's tender healing in other women.

Kesler, Jay. *Being Holy, Being Human.*

Labeled volume 13 in The Leadership Library, this book aims at ministerial leaders. I believe mature believers from every walk of life may benefit from its insightful teaching and powerful applications. Kesler quotes the late C. S. Lewis, "When a man is getting better, he understands more and more clearly the evil that is still left in him. When a man is getting worse, he understands his own badness less and less" (p. 14). Commenting on the holy – human paradox, Kesler challenges "...we're called to be holy, to provide an example of righteous living for those we lead. On the other hand, we're human, unable to completely live up to our calling. How can we be ourselves and make our inevitable mistakes – indeed, commit our inevitable sins – without seeing our ministries destroyed? *Every Christian leader is forced to come to terms with this dilemma* [emphasis mine]" (p. 15). This is a deep book and is recommended to those who hunger and thirst after righteousness.

Lovelace, Richard F. *Dynamics of Spiritual Life: An Evangelical Theology of Renewal.*

Exhaustive, but readable. Not for the novice, Lovelace traces the theology of the spiritual life. Explaining sin, he says "In its biblical definition, sin cannot be limited to isolated instances or patterns of wrongdoing; it is something much more akin to the psychological term *complex*: [his emphasis] an organic network of compulsive attitudes, beliefs and behavior deeply rooted in our alienation from God. Sin originated in the darkening of the human mind and heart as man turned from the truth about God to embrace a lie about him and consequently a whole universe of lies about his creation. Sinful thoughts, words and deeds flow from this darkened heart automatically and compulsively, as water from a polluted fountain" (p. 88). Insightful.

MacArthur, John, Jr. *The Freedom and Power of Forgiveness.*

Another good study by an accomplished teacher of the Word of God. Highly recommended.

Miller, C. John. *Repentance & 20ᵗʰ Century Man.*

Biblical repentance has been dumbed-down to "simply changing your mind" by some authors. This grieves the Holy Spirit and robs a sinner from the true joy of real repentance. Miller, in few words (only 132 pages), pointedly uncovers the biblical doctrine of repentance. Crucial reading!

Shelly, Marshall. *Well-Intentioned Dragons.*

The first volume in *The Leadership Library* series, it focuses on how to minister to problem people in the church. The application of this key book is much broader. What about problem people in your extended family? Cutting edge quality, *Well-Intentioned Dragons* points to real solutions. What should you do with your dragon? Shelly suggests, "Pachomius has been largely forgotten in church history, but for modern-day believers beset by dragons, he can be adopted as a patron saint. He pointed out that as attractive as solitary sanctification may seem, it is life among the dragons that develops the qualities God requires" (p. 149). God gave us the Holy Spirit, not so we could circumvent the caustic, but so we could be the salt, light, ambassadors, and witnesses to them. Highly recommended!

Swindoll, Charles R. *Three Steps Forward Two Steps Back.*

Swindoll asks and answers, "Why keep persevering? I'll tell you why. Because it is in the realistic arena that true character is forged out, shaped, tempered, and polished. Because it is there that the life of Jesus Christ is given the maximum opportunity to be reproduced in us, replacing a thin fragile internal theology with a tough, reliable set of convictions that enable us to handle life rather than escape from it. What do believers need? Swindoll responds, "...*we need what perseverance offers:* [emphasis his] willingness to accept whatever comes, strength to face it head on, determination to stand firm, and insight to see the Lord's hand in it all. Without it, we stumble and fall. And God is grieved. With it, we survive and conquer. And God is glorified" (pp. 186–187). Highly recommended.

Wright, H. Norman. *How To Have A Creative Crisis.*

Wright rightly writes, "Crisis is not always bad. It can become a turning point in your life for the better" (cover). Sometimes a person must be flat on their back before they will look up. As unusual as it sounds, crises can be anticipated and you may plan ahead on how you will react to them. Author Jay E. Adams calls this "proacting" instead of reacting. Wright tells a story about a teacher who was faced with impending retirement, and pro-acted by expanding his interests and taking preparatory college courses. Explains Wright, "Since there would be a significant loss in his life – his job and his livelihood – he planned in advance for a variety of replacements and worked through some of those feelings of loss. By anticipating what was to come he eliminated the possibility of the transition becoming a crisis" (pp. 39–40). Practical book!

Bibliography

Adams, Jay E. *The Biblical View of Self-Esteem, Self-Love, Self-Image.* Eugene: Harvest House, 1986.
—Translator and Editor. *The Christian Counselor's New Testament.* Revised Edition. Hackettstown: Timeless Texts, 1994.
—*From Forgiven to Forgiving.* Amityville: Calvary Press, 1994.
—*Marriage, Divorce, And Remarriage In The Bible.* Phillipsburg: Presbyterian and Reformed, 1980.
—*Shepherding God's Flock.* Grand Rapids: Baker, 1979.

Anderson and Miller. *Leading Teens To Freedom In Christ.* Regal, 1977.

Baker, Jason D. *Parents' Computer Companion: A Guide to Software and Online Resources.* Grand Rapids: Baker, 1999.

Basch, Reva. *Researching Online For Dummies.* Foster City: IDG, 1998. [Includes CD-ROM].

Bloem, Diane Brummel. *A Woman's Workshop On Proverbs.* Grand Rapids: Lamplighter, 1978.
—With Robert C. Bloem. *A Woman's Workshop On Bible Marriages.* Grand Rapids: Lamplighter, 1980.

Boone, Shirley. *One Woman's Liberation.* New York: Bantam, 1972.

Burkett, Larry. *Your Finances In Changing Times.* USA: Campus Crusade for Christ, 1975.
—*Debt-Free Living.* Chicago: Moody, 1989.

Buzzell, Sid. General Editor. *The Leadership Bible.* Grand Rapids: Zondervan, 1998.

Carson, Donald A. *The Inclusive Language Debate: A Plea for Realism.* Grand Rapids: Baker, 1998.

Elliot, Elizabeth. *Let Me Be A Woman.* Wheaton: Tyndale, 1976.

Fitzpatrick, Elyse and Carol Cornish. *Women Helping Women.* Eugene: Harvest House, 1997.

Gallagher, Steve. *Tearing Down The High Places Of Sexual Idolatry.* Crittenden: Pure Life, 1986.

George, Elizabeth. *A Woman After God's Own Heart.* Eugene: Harvest House, 1997.
—*Beautiful in God's Eyes.* Eugene: Harvest House, 1998.
—*Women Who Loved God.* Eugene: Harvest House, 1999.

Gingrich, F. Wilbur and Frederick W. Danker. *A Greek-English Lexicon of the New Testament and Other Early Christian Literature.* 2nd ed. Revised and Augmented from Walter Bauer's 5th ed., 1958. Chicago: The University of Chicago Press, 1979.

Heald, Cynthia. *Loving your Husband*. Colorado Springs: Navpress, 1989.

Hromas, Roberta. *52 Simple Ways To Teach Your Child To Pray*. Nashville: Oliver Nelson, 1991.

Hsu, Jeffrey. *Computer Bible Study*. Dallas: Word, 1993.

Huggins, Kevin and Landrum, Phil. *Guiding Your Teen To A Faith That Lasts: A Blueprint For Building A Relationship With God*. Grand Rapids: Discovery, 1994.

Jenkins, Jerry B. editor. *Families: Practical Advice From More Than 50 Experts*. Chicago: Moody, 1993.

Johnson, Albert J. *A Christian Guide To Family Finances*. Wheaton: Victor, 1983.

Johnson, Rex. *At Home With Sex*. Wheaton: Victor, 1979.

Keller, W. Phillip. *A Layman Looks At The Love Of God: A New Devotional Study Of 1 Corinthians 13*. Minneapolis: Bethany, 1984.

Kesler, Jay. *Being Holy, Being Human*. Carol Stream: co-published by Christianity Today, and Word, The Leadership Library, Vol. 13, 1988.

Kuyper, Abraham. *Women Of The New Testament*. Grand Rapids: Daybreak, 1962.

Levine, John R. and Baroudi, Carol. *The Internet For Dummies*. San Mateo: IDG, 1993.

Lewis, C.S. *Mere Christianity*. Westwood: Barbour and Company, Inc. Reprint, Macmillan, 1952.

Lloyd-Jones, D. Martyn. *Spiritual Depression: Its Causes And Cure*. Grand Rapids: Eerdmans, 1965.

Lovelace, Richard F. *Dynamics Of Spiritual Renewal: An Evangelical Theology Of Renewal*. Downers Grove: Inter-Varsity, 1979.

Lovett, C. S. *Unequally Yoked Wives*. Baldwin Park: Personal Christianity, 1968.

MacArthur, John Jr. *Answering The Key Questions About The Family*. Panorama City: Word of Grace, 1984.
—*Different By Design*. Wheaton: Victor, 1994.
—*The Freedom And Power Of Forgiveness*. Wheaton: Crossway, 1998.
—*Successful Christian Parenting*. Nashville: Word, 1998.
—*Whose Money Is It Anyway?* Nashville: Word, 2000.

MacDonald, Gordon. *The Effective Father*. Wheaton: Tyndale, 1983.
—*Action Guide For Effective Fathers*. Wheaton: Tyndale, 1979.

Mack, Wayne A. *How To Develop Deep Unity In The Marriage Relationship.* Phillipsburg: Presbyterian and Reformed, 1977.

—*A Homework Manual For Biblical Counseling: Personal And Interpersonal Problems.* Vol. 1, Phillipsburg: Presbyterian and Reformed, 1980.

—*A Homework Manual For Biblical Counseling: Family And Marital Problems.* Vol. 2, Phillipsburg: Presbyterian and Reformed, 1980.

McManus, Michael J. *50 Practical Ways To Take Our Kids Back From The World.* Wheaton: Tyndale, 1993.

MacMillan, Buechner, and Webb. *Action Guide for The Effective Father.* Wheaton: Tyndale, 1979.

Miller, C. John. *Repentance And 20th Century Man.* Fort Washington: Christian Literature Crusade, 1995.

Missler, Nancy. *Why Should I Be The First To Change?* Coeur d'Alene: Koinonia, 1991.

Moulton, James Hope and George Milligan. *The Vocabulary of the Greek New Testament: Illustrated from the Papyri and Other Non-Literary Sources.* Grand Rapids: Eerdmans, 1972.

Palau, Luis. *The Only Hope For America: The Transforming Power Of The Gospel Of Jesus Christ.* Wheaton: Crossway, 1996.

Peace, Martha. *The Excellent Wife.* Focus, 1999.

Peel, Bill and Kathy. *Where Is Moses When We Need Him? Teaching Your Kids The Ten Values That Matter Most.* Nashville: Broadman & Holman, 1995.

Piper, John and Grudem, Wayne. Editors. *Recovering Biblical Manhood & Womanhood: A Response To Evangelical Feminism.* Wheaton: Crossway, 1991.

—*50 Crucial Questions About Manhood And Womanhood.* Libertyville: The Council on Biblical Manhood and Womanhood, 1992.

Polly, Jean Armour. *The Internet Kids & Family Yellow Pages, Third Edition.* Berkeley: Osborne/ McGraw-Hill, 1999 [Includes CD-ROM].

Pratt, Richard L. Jr. *Designed For Dignity.* Phillipsburg: Presbyterian and Reformed, 1993.

Price, Eugenia. *God Speaks To Women Today.* Grand Rapids: Zondervan, 1969.

Priolo, Lou. *The Complete Husband.* Amityville: Calvary Press, 1999.

Ray, Bruce A. *Withhold Not Correction.* Phillipsburg: Presbyterian and Reformed, 1978.

Roberts, Lee. *Praying God's Will For My Wife.* Nashville: Thomas Nelson, 1993.

Rosenberger, Margaret. *Issues In Focus: Gaining A Clear Biblical Perspective On The Complex Issues Of Our Time.* Ventura: Regal, 1989.

Ryrie, Charles Caldwell. *The Role Of Women In The Church.* Chicago: Moody, 1981.

Schultze, Quentin J. *Internet For Christians.* Muskegon: Gospel Films, 1995.

Shelley, Marshall. *Well-Intentioned Dragons.* Carol Stream: co-published by Christianity Today and Word, The Leadership Library, Vol. 1, 1988.

Smedes, Lewis B. *Sex For Christians.* Grand Rapids: Eerdmans, 1978.

Smith, Joyce Marie. *Esther: A Woman Of Courage.* Wheaton: Tyndale, 1984.

Smith, Kenneth G. and Floy M., *Learning To Be A Woman.* Downers Grove: Inter-Varsity, 1970.

Sweeting, George. *Love Is The Greatest.* Chicago: Moody, 1974.

Swindoll, Charles R. *Three Steps Forward, Two Steps Back: Preserving Through Pressure.* Nashville: Thomas Nelson, 1980.

Tada, Joni Eareckson. *Secret Strength.* Portland: Multnomah, 1988.

Thurman, Chris. *Self-Help Or Self-Destruction?* Nashville: Thomas Nelson, 1996.

Tripp, Paul David. *Age Of Opportunity: A Biblical Guide To Parenting Teens.* Phillipsburg: Presbyterian and Reformed, 1998.

Tripp, Tedd. *Shepherding A Child's Heart.* Wapwallopen: Shepherd, 1995.

Van Kooten, Tenis C. *Building The Family Altar.* Grand Rapids: Baker, 1969.

Wheat, Ed and Gaye. *Intended For Pleasure.* Old Tappan: Fleming H. Revell, 1981.

—*The First Years Of Forever.* Grand Rapids: Zondervan, 1988.

White, Jerry. *Honesty, Morality & Conscience.* Colorado Springs: Navpress, 1978.

—and Mary White. *The Christian in Mid-Life.* Colorado Springs: Navpress, 1978.

White, John. *Eros Defiled: The Christian And Sexual Sin.* Downers Grove: Inter-Varsity, 1979.

Wright, H. Norman. *Communication: Key To Your Marriage.* Glendale: Regal, 1980.

—*How To Have A Creative Crisis.* Waco: Word, 1986.

Wyrtzen, David. *Raising Worldly-Wise But Innocent Kids.* Grand Rapids: Discovery, 1995.

Zerwick, Max and Mary Grosvenor. *A Grammatical Analysis of the Greek New Testament.* Rome: Biblical Institute Press, 1984.

Zodhiates, Spiros. *To Love Is To Live.* Grand Rapids: Eerdmans, 1970.

Magazines, Booklets and Journals

Adams, Jay E."What Do You Do When" pamphlet series, includes "What Do You Do When Your Marriage Goes Sour?" "What Do You Do When Anger Gets The Upper Hand?" "What Do You Do When You Become Depressed?" "What Do You Do When Fear Overcomes You?" "What Do You Do When You Worry All The Time?" "What Do You Do When You Know That You're Hooked?," Phillipsburg: Presbyterian and Reformed, 1975.

—"Gaining An Accurate Self-Image," *The Journal Of Pastoral Practice*, Vol. VII, No. 1, 1984, 40–50.

Beck, Aaron T., M.D., "Why Husbands Won't Talk," condensed from *Love Is Never Enough*, cited in *Reader's Digest*. December 1988, 9–10,13,16.

Cooke, Stuart. "Glad You Asked," *Reader's Digest*. December 1988, 93.

Covey, Stephen R. "Why Character Counts: Without It You'll Never Truly Succeed," *Reader's Digest*. January 1999, 132–135.

Covington, Sharon B. "Book Reviews," on "Women Helping Women," *The Journal of Biblical Counseling*. Vol. 16, No. 1, Fall 1997.

Cowan and Kinder, "10 Secrets Happy Couples Share," In *Women Men Love/ Women Men Leave*, *Reader's Digest*. June 1988, 197–202.

Crenshaw, Nadine. "How To Find True Love," *Reader's Digest*. May 1991, 33–36.

Farris, Joseph. Cartoon, *Leadership: A Practical Journal For Church Leaders*, Vol. XIX, No. 4, Fall 1998, 125.

Forrey, Jeffery S. "Christian Communication," *The Journal Of Biblical Counseling*. Vol. 16, No. 2, Winter 1998, 37–41.

Fulcher, Marlene R. "Life In The United States," *Reader's Digest*. December 1993.

Gifford, Susan Korones. "22 Ways To Pamper Your Marriage," *Redbook*. May 1997, 73–74, 86.

Henry, J. Gordon. "Words," *Reflector*. Vol. 44 No. 3, Fall-Winter 1998, 6.

"In Brief," *Christianity Today*. 8 February 1999, 11.

Komarnicki, Kristyn. "FATHERHOOD: At-Home Dads Gather and Bond," *Christianity Today*. 11 January 1999, 13.

MacArthur, John. "Shade For The Children," *Masterpiece*. Summer 1992, 4–9.

Maddox, Marisela. "The Shortest Marriage," *World*. 19 December 1999, 23.

Morice, Laura. "Marriage Resolutions For The New Year," *Reader's Digest*. January 1999, 158–162.

"The No-Comment Zone-Montana," *World*. 9 January 1999, 11.

Orecklin, Michele. "Diary of a Marriage," *Time*. 19 April, 1999, 91.

Phillips, Holly. "How Can Men And Women Connect?" (*Men Of Integrity: Your Daily Guide To The Bible And Prayer,* 2 January 1999), *Promise Keepers*. January-February 1999.

Piper, John. *Christianity Today,* cited by Jay E. Adams in *The Journal Of Pastoral Practice*. Vol. VII, No.1, 41–50.

Soto, Karen. "Humor In Uniform," *Reader's Digest*. January 1999, 93.

"Truth (2 Cor. 13:8)," *Leadership: A Practical Journal For Church Leaders*. Vol. XX, No. 1, Winter 1999, 75.

Audio and Video Tapes

Lewis, Robert M. *Men's Fraternity*. Little Rock: Fellowship Bible Church.

Tripp, Paul David. A*ge Of Opportunity: A Biblical Guide To Parenting Teens*. SDG Communications, 1998.

Wheat, Ed, M.D., *Love-Life For Every Married Couple*. Springdale: Scriptural Counsel, 1979.

Wheat, Gaye. *Sex For Married Women*. Springdale: Scriptural Counsel, 1990.

Newspapers

Brothers, Joyce. "I Love You: Know What I Mean?" *New York Daily News*. 3 June 1989, 39.

Landers, Ann. "Love – Or Its Kissing Cousin," New York: Dailey News. 3 June 1989, 10.

Riley, Michael. "No God? No Problem: American Atheists Fight For The Right Not To Believe," *Home News Tribune*. 28 January 1999, D1–2.

Endnotes

Introduction

1   Marisela Maddox, "The Shortest Marriage?," *World* Magazine, December 19, 1998, p. 23.
2   Michele Orecklin, "Diary of a Marriage," *Time*, April 19, 1999, p. 91.
3   Laura Morice, "Marriage Resolutions for the New Year," *Readers' Digest,* January 99, pp. 158–162.
4   Stephen R. Covey, "Why Character Counts: Without it, You'll Never Truly Succeed," *Reader's Digest*, January 1999, pp. 132–135.

Study One – Foundations for Marriage

5   Luis Palau, *The Only Hope for America: The Transforming Power of the Gospel of Jesus Christ* (Wheaton: Crossway Books, 1996), p. 164.
6   Ibid. pp. 164–169.
7   Connell Cowan and Melvin Kinder, *Women Men Love/Women Men Leave* (New York: Clarkson N. Potter, Inc., 1987) quoted in *Reader's Digest*, June 1988, pp. 197–202.

Study Two – Love

8   Joyce Brothers, "I Love You: Know What I Mean?," *Daily News*, June 3, 1989, p. 39.
9   Ann Landers, "Love – or its Kissing Cousin," *Daily News*, June 3, 1989, p. 10.
10 F. Wilbur Gingrich and Frederick W. Danker, *A Greek-English Lexicon of the New Testament and Other Early Christian Literature, Second Edition.* (Chicago: The University of Chicago Press, 1979) p. 859. Revised and augmented from Walter Bauer's Fifth Edition, 1958.
11 Bauer, p. 311.

Study Three – Perception and Sensitivity

12 James Hope Moulton and George Milligan, *The Vocabulary of the Greek New Testament: Illustrated from the Papyri and Other Non-Literary Sources* (Grand Rapids: Eerdmans, 1972), p. 669.
13 John Piper, *Christianity Today*, August 1977, quoted by Jay E. Adams, *Journal of Pastoral Practice*, Vol. VII, No. 1, 40– 50.
14 Matthew McKay and Patrick Fanning, *Self-Esteem* (New York: St. Martin's Press, 1987), quoted by Chris Thurman, *Self-Help or Self-Destruction?* (Nashville: Thomas Nelson, 1996), pages 23–27.

15   J. I. Packer, *Keep in Step with the Spirit* (Old Tappan: Revell, 1984), quoted by Jay E. Adams, *The Biblical View of Self-Esteem, Self-Love, Self-Image* (Eugene: Harvest House, 1986), p. 94.

Study Four – Communication

16   Marlene R. Fulcher, "Life in these UNITED STATES," *Reader's Digest*, December 1993, p. 81.

17   *Men of Integrity: Your Daily Guide to the Bible and Prayer,* January/February 1999, Promise Keepers, Saturday, January 2.

18   Aaron T. Beck, "Why Husbands Won't Talk," *Reader's Digest*, December 1988, p. 13.

19   Jeffery S. Forrey, "Christian Communication," *Journal of Biblical Counseling*, Winter 1998, pp. 37–41.

Study Seven – Children and Parenting

20   John F. MacArthur, Jr., *Masterpiece*, Summer 1992, pp. 4–9.

21   Stuart Cooke, "Glad You Asked," *Reader's Digest,* December 1988.

22   Michael Riley, *Home News Tribune,* January 28, 1999, D1–D2.

23   "The No-Comment Zone," *World*, January 9, 1999, p. 11.

Study Eight – Marital Roles, Relationships, and Responsibilities

24   Karen Soto, "Humor in Uniform," *Reader's Digest*, January 1999, p. 93.

25   Kristyn Komarnicki, "At-Home Dads Gather and Bond," *Christianity Today,* January 11, 1999, p.13.

26   Donald A. Carson, *The Inclusive Language Debate: A Plea for Realism* (Grand Rapids: Baker, 1998), p. 199.

Study Nine – Our Money

27   Roderick E. Huron, compiler, *Christian Minister's Manual* (Cincinnati: Standard Publishing, 1984), p.106.

Study Ten – Conflict Resolution

28   J. Gordon Henry, "Words," *Reflector*, Fall–Winter 1998, p. 6.

29   Adapted from the teachings of Jay E. Adams.

30   Susan Gifford, "22 Ways to Pamper Your Marriage," *Redbook*, May 1997, p. 74.

Appendix 1: The Equality of Women

31 Carson, p. 199.

Appendix 2: What About Divorce and Remarriage

32 Nadine Crenshaw, "How to Find True Love," *Reader's Digest*, May 1991, pp. 33–36.
33 Bauer, p. 693.
34 Max Zerwick and Mary Grosvenor, *A Grammatical Analysis of the Greek New Testament* (Rome: Biblical Institute Press, 1984), p. 61.